TOP TEN SELLING

How Sales Professionals in the Top 10% get there...and stay!

The Lumberjack Chronicles

DAN NORMAN
Edited by Jack Roth

Top Ten Selling and Publishing
Celebration, Florida

TOP TEN SELLING

How Sales Professionals in the Top 10% get there...and stay!

The Lumberjack Chronicles
By Dan Norman

Edited by Jack Roth

Copyright © 2007 Dan Norman
First edition, 2007

All rights reserved.
No part of this publication may be reproduced, distributed or transmitted in any form or by any means, including photocopying, recording, or other electronic or mechanical methods or by any information storage and retrieval system without the prior written permission of the publisher, except in the case of brief quotations embodied in critical review and certain other non-commercial uses permitted by copyright law.

Published by:
Top Ten Selling and Publishing
P.O. Box 470416
Celebration, Florida 34747

Printed in the United States of America

Cover design: www.TheBookProducer.com, Tulsa OK
Inside Layout: www.TheBookProducer.com, Tulsa OK
Printed by: DeHart's Media Services

ISBN-13: 978-0-9798151-0-2
ISBN-10: 0-9798151-0-x

Dedication

This book is dedicated to the thousands of sales representatives, hundreds of sales managers and dozens of sales directors that I have had the pleasure of working with throughout my career. A special dedication is extended to the more than 300 Top 10% Sales Professionals who were kind enough to spend time with me, put up with my endless questions and share the reasons for their extraordinary success. Without them this book would have only been about three pages long…maybe four!

Table of Contents

Chapter 1	The Lumberjacks Taught Me to Sell!	7
Chapter 2	"You Are Under Arrest for Assaulting an Officer with an Egg McMuffin® "	23
Chapter 3	I Always Knew You Were the Crazy One of My Boys!	31
Chapter 4	The Attributes and Practices of the Best	39
Chapter 5	The Character of the Best Salespeople	43
Chapter 6	The Mindset of the Very Best!	53
Chapter 7	Expectations of the Very Best	63
Chapter 8	Self-Education Practices of the Very Best	75
Chapter 9	Sales Actions of the Very Best Salespeople	81
Chapter 10	The Customer Experience Commitment of the Top 10 Percent	97
Chapter 11	Why Are the Best Motivated to Be So Successful? . .	105
Chapter 12	So What?	109
About the Author		111

The Lumberjacks Taught Me to Sell!

My career in sales began in a logging camp high in the hills of North Georgia. Fresh out of college with a Bachelor of Fine Arts degree in Painting and Drawing, I was making my first sales call as a sales representative with Motorola. Locked in my car, dressed in a suit and surrounded by lumberjacks wielding running chain saws above their heads, I was afraid to open the door. (Yes, that's right … lumberjacks! That job is rated the worst in America according to The Jobs Rated Almanac by Les Krantz.) Not only was I afraid of my customers (chain saw massacre movies); I knew very little about how to sell anything.

My original career aspiration was to become a comic strip artist. I was an excellent illustrator and could always make people laugh. I combined these two talents early in life as a fifth grader in Catholic school and had quite a following for my comic book about my teachers – Sister Anne Marie and Sister Elizabeth. The story line was about a pair of Catholic nuns who got in all kinds of trouble around the rectory after routinely having too much wine during communion. My career as a young author was cut short, however, when my scorned fourth-grade girlfriend blew the whistle on me during recess. The original copy of *Nutty Nuns of Saint Bridget's* was confiscated by Sister Anne Marie herself and ripped to pieces in front of the class. She was my first critic, although she never read a word of the comic book. To this day I believe she would have appreciated the part about Sister Elizabeth and she impersonating two of the Wise Men statues in the life-sized nativity scene on the lawn of the church.

Years later, while in college, I submitted any number of comics to the newspaper syndicates, but the competition was fierce. I either did not hear back from them or got a letter that read, "You are a talented and potentially successful comic strip artist, but we have no interest at this time." New comic strips in the newspaper didn't appear to be as good as mine, and most of them were written by people who were not really comic strip artists.

> *The Daily Exaggeration* is happy to now feature the comic strip of Judge Howie Cheatem, a successful civil court judge turned comic strip artist. Judge Cheatem brings his hilarious antics on the night court bench tossing ne'er-do-wells into the hoosegow to the comic pages of the *Exaggeration*. The comic features a squirrel, (Judge Jimmie-Bob), a talking apple (the bailiff) and two farm animals (the defense and prosecuting attorneys). Please join the *Exaggeration* in welcoming the Judge and his crazy characters to our comic strip line up.

It was obvious that a funny and classically educated artist and illustrator had no business attempting to become a comic strip artist. I didn't have a law degree! Apparently, I needed a job both to pay my bills *and* save money to go to law school in order to become a comic strip artist.

OK sorry to digress. Now back to my first sales call in the hills of North Georgia – Locked in my car, dressed in a suit and surrounded by lumberjacks carrying chain saws, I was afraid to open the door ...

Should I open the door or just drive away? Unsure of what to do at that exact moment, I fell into a trance, reflecting on the chain of events that had brought me to this horror show. I felt misled by my manager and training instructor. I was told that I was to be a communications consultant in the pulpwood industry. During three weeks of training I was taught to sell two-way radio systems, closed circuit television security equipment, beepers, mobile telephones and hand-held walkie-talkies. There were pictures of astronauts carrying little walkie-talkies on the moon, doctors talking on mobile phones while driving their Mercedes Benz to their beautiful homes, police officers using closed-circuit television to catch thieves in convenience stores. All of the Motorola communications consultants in the videos were wearing suits and ties and driving long, colorful, deluxe-edition company cars. And here I sat in my beige Chevy Nova about to be ripped out of my car and turned into pulpwood. This was *not* what I envisioned.

I had business cards that read "Communications Consultant – Pulpwood Industry," but I didn't feel like a communications consultant in the pulpwood industry. I wore a suit like the guys in the videos and was ready to sell walkie-talkies to astronauts. I hadn't signed up for this. It's all about expectations, and to better help you understand mine, let's go back to the night before my first sales call.

After I completed my training, Motorola moved me to Rome, a small town nestled in the hills of North Georgia. Contrary to what you might think, Rome wasn't quite off of the beaten path, but it did appear to me that the part of the path that was beaten was the part being used by those trying to get out!

I spent my first night in Rome going through files of existing customers in the area. Only 47 files existed, and all of the customer names sounded very similar: BRS Pulpwood Company, Johnnie Putnam d/b/a/ Johnnie Putnam Pulpwood & Logging Company, Willie D. Smith Hauling and 44 similar versions of what appeared to be pulpwood companies. It seemed a bit odd that none of the 47 companies had a business address. They all had post office boxes.

The next morning I started making telephone calls beginning with the first one in the file and called AAA Pulpwood Company. "I ain't in right now. Leave a message at the beep."

I did. In fact, I left about 20 messages that morning on various answering machines, dialed 10 or more numbers that just rang and left a few messages with answering services. During lunch, I decided to drive north a bit and look for paper mills, which is what I thought a pulpwood company was. That afternoon I made sales calls to several lumber yards and what appeared to be a paper mill. Those first calls did not go well.

I would introduce myself and say, "You don't want to buy any two-way radios, do you?"

The managers of the yards all said "NO" and then just gazed at me with a puzzled look while tilting their heads from side to side. You know the look. You've seen your dog look at you that way when you ask him to vacuum the house or fix dinner, or some other impossible task like not relieve himself on the living room rug.

On my fourth day, and my third day of driving around the outskirts of town, my manager called me on the two-way radio in my car to see how I was doing. Sorry, but I just have to stop here and comment on a point.

It's not that I thought I was better than everyone else at Motorola, but I could never get used to talking on a two-way radio. I wasn't a truck driver, for crying out loud! I was a "Communications Consultant – Pulpwood Industry."

Anyway, my boss would call me and say something like, "MG-1 to MG-27, what is your 10-20?"

I would respond with, "10-4, MG-1 this is MG-27 and my 10-20 is Resaca." (This is radio talk for, "Hi Wayne, this is Dan and I'm in Resaca.)

Once we got through all of the preliminary "10-speak," I told him I was driving around Calhoun and Resaca looking for paper mills because none of them would answer their phones. He calmly explained that my customers were pulpwooders, not paper mills.

So naturally I asked, "What is a pulpwooder?"

He lost his calm tone and barked into his two-way radio, "Lumberjacks, loggers!"

I asked, "How do I find them? All of the addresses are post office boxes!"

He roared, "I guess you need to drive around until you see one of those logging trucks hauling cut-down trees with red rags tied on the ends of the logs. Watch to see where it came out of the woods or wait until you see empty ones going the other way. Then, follow one of them up in to the woods to the logging camp."

The Lumberjacks Taught Me to Sell!

CMB Pulpwood Company was the name on the side of the first logging truck I ever followed up a dirt road into a logging camp. I remember the drive like it was yesterday. Sunlight filtering through the trees, the only sound was the roar of the logging truck engine as it plowed up the hill churning dust in its path. I followed it deeper and deeper into the woods wondering if I should turn back. The truck finally pulled up into a clearing with me behind it, and I saw that the camp was filled with other trucks and dozens of loggers. When they saw my car appear from the dust storm created by the truck, they all hid behind trees. I felt like I was in the scene from the *Wizard of Oz* when Dorothy's house fell out of the sky, landed in Munchkin land and all the little people hid behind trees giggling at her. I had no idea why they were all hiding or what to do next!

So, there I was in my beige Chevy Nova with a "public safety" radio antenna on top wearing a black suit, a black tie and a white shirt. As I got out of the car, one of the loggers was pushed forward from behind the trees. Obviously he was picked by the others to find out who I was. He eased forward slowly and began to shuffle over. He looked like the banjo kid's grandfather from the movie *Deliverance*.

He stopped shuffling about 10 feet away form me and said, *"Yoo ah govmen revnewer?"*

I didn't understand a word he said, but it sounded like a threat so I said, "No sir," hurried back to my car, locked the doors and fumbled to get my keys in the ignition while two or three loggers emerged from behind the trees and began circling my car with chain saws.

Two months later at a Waffle House in Calhoun, Charles "Chuck" Michael Brown, the owner of CMB Pulpwood Company, explained to me why they were hiding.

"When you pulled up in that government-looking car, in a coat and tie, the crew went to hidin' because they thought that you was a revenuer, a federal agent who busts up moonshine stills," he said. "Or worse yet an income tax collector."

Meanwhile, back at the logging camp, I finally got my car started and backed all the way down the dirt road, dodging pulpwood trucks coming up the road into the camp.

After backing down the road, I went straight back to my home office to call my boss and tell him that I wasn't cut out for this kind of selling and that I was better suited selling mobile phones and beepers to smiling doctors and two-way radios to NASA astronauts.

His response was much like you would have expected it to be: "There are probably 10 doctors in Rome if you count the veterinarian, and the closest thing to an astronaut that you're gonna find will be some delusional drunk at the New Faces Lounge next to the Holiday Inn by the community airport."

He went on to say he didn't care who I sold to, I just needed to make cold calls and sell Motorola's products. He did, however, feel that my best opportunity was selling two-way radios to lumberjacks, as the pulpwood industry was thriving in North Georgia. So, after listening to his advice, the next day I developed a plan. The plan was to sell mobile phones and beepers to every doctor, dentist, lawyer and business owner who I could find in the towns of North Georgia.

I put my comic strip artistic skills to use by creating my own flyers. I had them printed and mailed to every professional in town. A week later I hadn't received a single phone call! I double checked the phone number on the flyer, but it was correct. I thought perhaps the comic strips hadn't been the best approach and that I needed to be more professional. I began making phone calls to schedule appointments. All of the receptionists and assistants were very nice, but I received no return calls.

The following week I received a greeting card from my boss with a hangman's noose on the front of it. Inside the card was printed, "Just a reminder that you are responsible for increasing sales!" It was signed by my boss.

Later that week I received a call from my neighboring "Motorola Communications Consultant – Pulpwood Industry" in Chattanooga, Tennessee. He told me a man named Charles "Chuck" Michael Brown of CMB Pulpwood Company in Calhoun had called him. Mr. Brown bought a new logging truck and called the Motorola office in Chattanooga to find out how much a two-way truck radio would cost. Mr. Brown was told that the communications consultant from Rome would call him back.

The Lumberjacks Taught Me to Sell!

If you're in the sales profession, you've probably already been trained on the assumptive close. In fact, most of you are probably very good at it. The principle behind the "assumptive close" technique is that you attempt to complete or "close" a sale by assuming as though the customer has already made the decision to buy! Hence, it's called the "assumptive close." For example, let's say you're a car salesman. You've talked to a customer on the phone about a brand new Pontiac Aztec that you have at your car dealership. The car has everything the customer wants, and she is coming in that afternoon to test drive it. By the time she arrives, the car has been serviced, washed and her name is prominently displayed on a huge "sold" tag that covers the entire windshield. You've completed the order form, and all she needs to do is sign it. She sees the car, is overwhelmed with its beauty, signs the order, jumps in the car and does *Dukes of Hazard* doughnuts in the parking lot before tearing into traffic.

Well, I didn't do it that well! After I learned that Mr. Brown needed a two-way radio for his new logging truck, I decided to practice the "assumptive close" as I learned to do it in sales school. I wrote up an order form ready for his signature and began calling to make an appointment to go see him. He was out in the field a lot so I left several messages on his answering machine asking him to call me. A couple of days passed and I still hadn't heard back from Mr. Brown, but the completed order was on the corner of my desk, ready for a signature, so I kept calling. While I was at lunch the following day, our office assistant saw the order, assumed that I had finally sold something and processed the order for shipment. Off and on over the next week I continued to leave messages and play phone tag with Mr. Brown. We never actually spoke, much less scheduled an appointment.

Unknown to me, the two-way radio was delivered the following week along with an invoice for $1,200.

My phone rang. It was Mr. Brown. He said one thing, "Meet me at the Waffle House in Calhoun at 11 a.m.!"

"Yes, sir," I said.

I couldn't find the order I had written up, but I figured I would write a new one when I got there. I jumped into my car and headed for Calhoun. I realized within a few minutes I had forgotten to ask which Waffle House in Calhoun, but I comforted myself by thinking, "How many could there be?" It's a known fact that there are more Waffles Houses than Baptist churches in some communities in Georgia. Such was the case in Calhoun. Standing in front of the first Waffle House I went to, I could actually see two more of them, but only one church. I was 30 minutes late before I found a Waffle House with a CMB Pulpwood Company truck parked out front. I walked in with my hand outstretched and a big smile on my face. Now remember that I didn't know the order had been mistakenly processed, let alone that Mr. Brown had already received the two-way radio along with an invoice. I thought I was meeting him to make my first sale.

In fact, I didn't even know what Mr. Brown looked like and had introduced myself to three people before he stood and said, "Hey, over here!"

I walked over, shook his hand, introduced myself, reached for a business card and was about to sit down when suddenly he got up and walked out. I stood there watching through the window as he went to his truck, opened the passenger door, pulled out a Motorola box, walk to my beige Chevy Nova and deposited the box on the hood of my car, firmly. Then he stormed back inside, handed me a piece of paper that appeared to be an invoice from Motorola and started back out of the door.

At that point the waitress shouted, "Chuck, here's your bill!"

To which Chuck replied, "The Motorola man is paying it."

As he passed my car, I guess he didn't feel like he had deposited the Motorola box on my hood firmly enough because he picked it up and deposited it a bit more firmly, twice. Then he got in his truck and drove away.

Inside, a deathly hush came over the crowd. No one was eating. There were two waitresses standing dumbstruck behind the counter in the "order-yelling spot" but not yelling orders to the cook. Even the cook had stopped – mid-waffle – to see what was going on. Everyone was quiet and all were staring, wide-eyed, open-mouthed, forks of hash browns midway between plates and mouths, directly at me.

The Lumberjacks Taught Me to Sell!

I was the object of everyone's attention and could think of nothing to say to ease the tension except, "Looks like you need to make sure his eggs are cooked right next time!"

No one laughed. At this point I realized not only was I a bad salesperson, but I was an even worse stand-up comedian. Embarrassed, with sweat breaking out on my forehead, I paid the bill and left as quickly as I could. Once I was in my car and away from the scene, I pieced it all together – the order form that had disappeared from my desk, the Motorola box, the invoice. It suddenly all made sense.

The next day, now having a real address for CMB Pulpwood Company on the packing slip from the box, I went to see Mr. Brown to apologize. He wasn't home, but his wife and three dogs were. I apologized and asked Mrs. Brown to please pass my apologies to Mr. Brown. She promised to do so, and early the next morning I got a call from Mr. Brown.

"Guess you got a two-way radio that was returned that I'm gonna be able to buy real cheap now, huh?" he said. "Meet me at the Waffle House at 11:00 am."

So, let's recap. After three and a half months I had made only one sale … and it had been the result of a mistake. My future as a sales representative wasn't looking good, and the next Monday morning it got worse. I was getting into my car to go to the office and make some phone calls when my boss called over the radio and said, "Dan, come to Atlanta today."

I knew I was in trouble because he didn't start the conversation with "MG-1 to MG-27" or any other "10-speak." On the drive from Rome to Atlanta I had plenty of time to think. I was sure I was going to be fired. I was just out of college, had a new baby girl and was going to be broke and stuck in Rome for the rest of my life. It was a miserable trip. It was rainy and cold and the traffic was very heavy as I neared Atlanta. I had no idea what I was going to do. Maybe he would give me one more chance. I dismissed that thought quickly after remembering the note he sent me two weeks earlier that read, "Sell something!" and had a McDonald's job application stapled to it.

I started thinking about how hard I worked to try and sell something. I tried to reach all of the existing customers by phone to see if they needed anything or knew anyone who did. I was on the phone calling doctors and lawyers constantly trying to get an appointment. I started planning my defense. No one wanted this stuff. Our two-way radios, beepers and phones were too expensive. The competition was much cheaper. They had more features and local repair service too. Their sales reps had nicer company cars and bigger expense accounts so they could take customers to lunch and buy them dinner.

I tried everything. I spent hours creating the flyer I mailed out to every professional in town. It was a great flyer with two great drawings of guys in cars. One of them was all frazzled, obviously trying to get somewhere. The other was reading his beeper, talking on the phone and smiling. They were really good drawings!

It's funny how the mind can play tricks on you when you focus on something long enough. As I was thinking how hard I worked on the flyer, the thought suddenly dawned on me that maybe my boss had seen it. That's it! He saw the flyer and sent it to the marketing department as an example of how to use direct mail advertising to sell our products. They must have loved it. By the time I was near the Atlanta office, I convinced myself they were going to promote me and put me in the marketing department.

I entered the building all smiles, saying hello to everyone. I hadn't seen any of them for three and a half months, and they all wanted to know how I was doing up in Rome. It took about 15 minutes to get back to my boss's office because I had to stop and say hello to everyone. I knocked on his door, walked in, said hello, shook his hand and started to sit down.

"Don't bother to sit," he said. "If you don't sell something within two weeks I'm gonna fire your ass. Now get outta here."

I suddenly got the Waffle House sweats again like when Charles "Chuck" Michael Brown of CMB pulpwood Company yelled at me. I turned, left his office and stood outside his door trying to think of what to do next. I couldn't just leave right away. It had taken me 15 minutes to get through the building while saying hello to everyone. If they saw me leaving so quickly they would think I must be in trouble. They would be right. I was in trouble! So I hid in the men's room for 10 minutes sitting in a stall, sweating and wondering where I was going to get a job in Rome. I wondered what I had done with that McDonald's application. I finally mustered the courage to leave the men's room, made a respectable exit, got in my car and began the long drive back to Rome.

The next day I called my boss, told him I wanted to keep my job and asked him for some advice?

"You need to make cold calls, face-to-face cold calls," he said. "Don't make anymore phone calls and don't create any more flyers. Good drawings by the way! Get in your car with the yellow pages and make face-to-face cold calls on lumberjacks! I promise you if you make 20 cold calls a day, you'll make so many sales that I'll be promoting you in a year."

I still had some doubts in my mind about cold calling lumberjacks in the woods. I was sure the really successful Motorola communications consultants must secretly have advertising support and a room full of telemarketing sales representatives sending them leads. So I decided to call some of the really successful sales people at Motorola and ask what they did to make so many sales. I called John Brooks in Gainesville, Ga. We trained together, and the sales reports showed he was doing very well. He said he made face-to-face cold calls on loggers, plumbers and construction companies all day long. He never went to the office and asked everyone if they knew anyone who might need two-way radios. Wayne Michaels, down in Tifton, Ga., said pretty much the same thing, although most of his cold calling was to farmers.

Even the king of sales, the guy who made it all look so easy, the guy with all of the posh Atlanta accounts, the No. 1 sales rep in the southeast region, Warren "the man" O-Toole, said, "Cold calls all day long on construction companies."

The next morning I left home with 20 business cards and a mission: Make 20 calls and give out 20 business cards before quitting for the day. Some days it was easy. I would stop at a plumbing company or wrecker service on the way to my now common-place drives up dirt roads looking for lumberjacks. I would be out of business cards by mid-afternoon. Other days it was much tougher. I would be at a gas station at 8 p.m. filling my tank and trying to get the guy at the next pump to take a card.

I remember late one evening talking to a plumber at the gas pumps of a 7-Eleven convenience store. I handed him my card and he said, "*Naw*, you ken keep *yur* card, I don't need *nunna dem* two-way *radyoos*."

To which I responded, "Please keep it. You might run into someone who does need two-way radios, and I would appreciate you passing along my card."

He said, "Okee dokee" and I thought I was done for the day until I saw him throw it in an ashtray on his way into the store. I retrieved it, got into my car and went to look for someone else to give my 20th business card to so I could go home.

Seven days after my trip to Atlanta (and 140 cold calls later), I got a call from "Sewer Sam the Plumbing Man" who was based in Rome. He said the owner of a local pest control company gave him my card at a Rotary Club meeting, and he wanted to talk to me about two-way radios for his trucks.

"Meet me at the Waffle House by the Holiday Inn at noon," he said.

I got to the Waffle House before him and saw him pull up in a pink van with "Here comes Sewer Sam the Plumbing Man!" written on the side. We ate, I talked, he signed and I made my first sales of a two-way radio system for his three trucks.

When I returned to the office to process the order, I had a message from a lumberjack named Raymond Thacker and one from Chuck (Mr. Brown). I called Chuck first and he told me he had passed my name along to his cousin, Raymond Thacker, who was also a logger, and told him he needed to get two-way radios.

The next day I met with Raymond Thacker of Raymond Thacker Hauling Company in the parking lot of the Cahutta Lodge near Ellijay, Ga. I thought I was going to meet Raymond, get an order signed and be the proud owner of two sales in two days, but it didn't go that smoothly. First, we were talking about two-way radios in freezing cold, windy, drizzly weather on top of a mountain in a parking lot. Second, the wet, steamy hood of my beige Chevy Nova was acting as my desk top and my brochures were sticking all over it. Third, Raymond was chewing tobacco and spitting into a Styrofoam coffee cup from Hardee's. And finally, it didn't appear that Raymond really wanted to buy any two–way radios. Two-way radios were expensive and Raymond said he couldn't imagine that spending that kind of money would help his business in any way.

"Dem is *spensive* and I *caint magin* that the base station will be able to talk to them up here on the mountain," he said. "I don't think that dog will hunt!"

A million thoughts passed through my mind, including: *It's cold as heck out here! Why is he calling two-way radios "dogs that won't hunt?" He almost missed the Styrofoam cup that time and spit on my shoe. What did I learn about how to handle objections like this in sales training? Oh yeah! Share appreciation for the customer's concern, rephrase the objection to expose the true concern, and turn it into a question you can then answer!*

What happened next happened very quickly. It was similar to what happened once at a birthday party I took my 5-year-old son to. The eight-month pregnant mother of the birthday boy, wearing a snug, blue maternity top no sooner opened the front door to her home when my son blurted out, "Wow daddy, she looks like the blue blow-up whale in our pool."

"We really can't stay," I said as I turned toward my car and simultaneously handed her the present.

"I understand!" she said as she closed the front door.

I can't remember the exact words I said to Raymond. I honestly think I immediately blocked it from my memory, refusing to believe I was capable of such nonsense. To the best of my knowledge it was something like, "I understand your concern. So you're worried that the base station won't be able to hunt ... uhhh ... I mean, talk ... to the spensive ... I mean, expensive dogs on the mountain?"

Raymond turned immediately and got into his truck while simultaneously spitting into his Hardee's cup. "Thanks *fer yur* time," he said. "Don't *bleeve* I need *em*!"

"I understand," I said as the truck passed, splashing water on my already soaking wet shoes. I remember thinking, *I really need more training on that one.*

The next day I was back following lumberjacks, handing out business cards and waiting for my boss to call and praise me for my sale to Sewer Sam. Eleven business cards into the day, I got a call from the office saying that I needed to meet Ronnie Williams at the Waffle House in Blue Ridge to give him prices for some new two-way radios. I met Mr. Williams a week earlier at a truck stop along US Hwy 41 and gave him a business card. At the time he wasn't a Motorola customer. He already had two-way radios, which he purchased from a competitor, in a few of his trucks. He wasn't thrilled with his sales representative, however, as he tried to get him to return his calls for weeks so he could order some new radios. Mr. Williams wanted 10 new units for his trucks and thought he would give Motorola a try. I thought I was dreaming. The problem was that he didn't have the money to buy the new radio equipment and had poor credit. This may have had some bearing on why his former sales rep was so hard to reach? Motorola wouldn't finance the equipment for him because of his credit. I suggested we go see a representative at his bank. I wasn't sure if two-way radios could be used as collateral on a loan like a car, but 10 radios were going to cost about as much as a car, so it was worth a try. As it turned out, the bank gave him a $15,000 loan using the two-way radio equipment as collateral.

As we left the bank Mr. Williams said, "*Goot* job Dave!"

"I'm Dan, not Dave, Mr. Williams," I said for about the 10th time.

He responded, "You *ken* use me as a *refernance* anytime you want. And … I will send all of the companies I work with *yer* way, Dave."

That was the turning point for my career in sales. Within a couple of months I had more calls coming in than I could imagine and half of them were referral's from existing customers. Anytime anyone called asking for Dave, I knew it was a referral from Mr. Williams. I thought about changing my name to Dave prompted by a call from one man. He called asking for Dave, and when I told him my name was Dan, not Dave, he said that Ronnie William's told him not to talk to anyone but Dave.

I found that by making as many cold calls as I could each day, I came across people who were ready to buy. They were too busy running their businesses to stop and look for sales representatives to meet their needs, but if you showed up at their door, you got their attention. I was still horrible at true selling skills such as interest creating introductions, cost justification, probing, overcoming objections and closing. I had, however, become very good at finding customers in the woods, explaining the benefits of two-way radios and following up on everything after the sale.

After I got to know my lumberjack customers better, I found they were good people after all. Some were a bit nasty looking, but any one of them would give you the shirt off his back if you needed it, and a couple of them had a habit of doing so whether you needed it or not. They were hard to find, and many were credit challenged and stubborn, but they bought a lot of two-way radios for all those logging trucks. To this day, I still get excited about the prospect of selling a bunch of two-way radios when I see one of those trucks on the highway with the red-tagged logs on the back.

"You Are Under Arrest for Assaulting an Officer with an Egg McMuffin®."

Note: Egg McMuffin® is a registered trademark of the McDonald's Corporation

I had become the "Cold Call King" of the Georgia region, making more cold calls than anyone else. And over the next year and a half I made more sales than anyone else as a result. I won every sales award that could be won in the region and on one occasion my boss asked me what I was doing up there to generate so much business.

"Twenty cold calls every day and referrals from existing customers," I said.

Unknown to my boss, the quality of my prospecting and cold calling left a lot to be desired. I was more concerned about finding sales I could close quickly than I was with developing long-term account potential. I wanted immediate sales, achievement and recognition. This was a short-term strategy with immediate high returns but not a good plan for development of accounts and sales in the long-run. In fact, I'm sure I sparked interest with a lot of potential customers, but with little to no follow-up, I'm sure I made my competitor's job a lot easier.

Regardless of how success is achieved, however, that achievement can often lead to advancement. This was the case for me. After only a year and a half at Motorola, with only a little more than a year of that time being productive and successful, I was promoted to management. I was given responsibility for four very successful and long-tenured sales representatives, but I was given almost no training on how to manage people.

All of my team members were in their mid- to late-30s and I was only 26. I wasn't well received as their manager. To make matters worse, I wasn't in the pulpwood industry anymore. I was promoted and moved into the government market with responsibility for managing a team selling products to police, fire and emergency rescue services. I knew little about long-term account development (as is required in the government marketplace), less about sales management and was unfamiliar with the products Motorola sold to the government market.

The first sales meeting I called was a disaster. I arrived at the Holiday Inn near the community airport early. It was so early they were still cleaning up the glasses and cigarettes from the previous night in the New Faces Lounge next door. I've always felt that a bar is a depressing place the morning after. Based on the looks of this one, I'm sure it was a depressing place the night before the morning after also. I'm also quite certain that based on the reputation of this establishment; there hadn't been a new face in the New Faces Lounge in a very long time.

I set up a flip chart that listed the sales quotas and my expectations of my team members. I prepared a binder for each of them that included the quotas and expectations as well as examples of the necessary forms and reports needed to be filled out each week and month. The scheduled meeting time (8 a.m.) came and went. No sales team.

I had another cup of coffee and at approximately 8:25 a.m. I revised my list of expectations, adding a new one: Be on time for all sales meetings!

At 8:35 a.m. I went outside to the parking lot. I'm not sure why people do that, but I did anyway. Wouldn't it seem logical that if the missing people were able to find the parking lot they would have been able to find their way into the building? I can't remember a single time when people I was expecting were late, and I went to the parking lot and found them out there saying, "Oh, thank heavens you came out here, we didn't know where to go to get inside or what to do next!"

"You Are Under Arrest for Assaulting an Officer with an Egg McMuffin®."

In this case, however, I did see something. I saw my team members coming out of the Waffle House across the street. I was overwhelmed and upset for two reasons. First of all, they went to the Waffle House instead of being on time to my first meeting. How disrespectful! Second, they didn't ask me. I love the Waffle House. I went back inside and waited, occasionally looking out the window to watch their progress. Ten minutes later, after cigarettes in the parking lot, a bathroom stop in the lobby and coffee in the restaurant, they arrived. Forty-five minutes late!

As they took their seats I began to get the feeling the meeting wasn't going to go well. It was obvious that each of them felt they were better qualified than me for the job. Truth be told, they were better qualified! Tommy Rainey was the most outspoken of the three. He was constantly getting up, revising my flip charts and reminding me of the fact that I didn't know the government marketplace.

At one point, when I was covering the mix of products we were expected to sell that year, Tommy blurted out, "Do you even know what a "wig-wag" is?"

"A wig what?" I asked.

"Well, if you don't know, I'm not gonna tell you," Tommy responded.

I returned with a brilliant, "Well, I don't care if you don't tell me."

At that moment, the meeting began to fall apart and resembled a third-grade math class of attention deficit disorder students just before lunch. The other three sales representatives were all talking at the same time; things were getting way out of hand.

Suddenly, Dave Parks asked, "Anyone hungry?"

Dead silence. Dave's suggestion was a good one, so we broke for lunch. My sales representatives presented forecasts for their accounts that afternoon, and it appeared we would not make the quotas I had assigned to them. They didn't appear to care!

Over the next few months, morale declined and we failed to achieve a single monthly quota. I asked my boss for advice. "Take control," he asserted. "You need to make certain they know who is boss. Make sure they know that they must make quota, and if they don't they'll be given an opportunity to succeed somewhere else."

I tried to become tough and straight forward. I felt I needed to make an example of someone. I sent a note out to my lowest-performing sales representative advising him that he needed to make quota. I even included a McDonald's application along with the note like my boss had once sent to me. I did, however, put a Post-it Note on the application that said, "Just kidding!" I got the application back four days later with my name and information printed in the blanks. He also attached a Post-it Note that read, "I'm kidding too!" I wasn't sure that he was.

One morning, during my fifth month as a sales manager, I was pulled over for speeding along I-75. I say "along" I-75 because I wasn't actually on I-75. I was on the entrance ramp getting back on I-75. I was on my way to Albany to conduct my monthly sales meeting and had stopped at a McDonald's at the Ashburn, Ga., exit. I was getting back on the highway with coffee, hash browns and McMuffin in hand.

Anyone familiar with South Georgia along I-75 knows the Ashburn exit is the one with the huge peanut monument on the side of the highway. That monument has the distinction of actually being the world's largest peanut, and it has greeted folks passing up and down I-75 for more than 30 years. So, there I was, sunlight glinting off of the great peanut, getting on the entrance ramp to get back on the highway when a police car pulled me over. The officer walked up to my car and asked me if I knew how fast I was going?

Why do police officers always ask you if you know how fast you were going? They know you're going to say, "About (insert the appropriately low speed here) officer." Then the officer will say, "I clocked you at (insert ridiculously high speed here) and I need to see your license and registration, please!"

So, when the officer asked me if I knew how fast I was going, I said, "Couldn't have been more than 40 as I'm still on the entrance ramp, officer.

"You Are Under Arrest for Assaulting an Officer with an Egg McMuffin®."

"Well, I clocked you at 90, and that's a dangerous speed for the highway let alone the entrance ramp," he said. "Please step outta the car."

At this point, the officer opened my door, grabbed my arm and pulled me, breakfast in hand, out of the car.

We all know there's an equal but opposite reaction to every action. The action, in this case, was me being pulled out of the car. The reaction was my Egg McMuffin flying out of my hand and exploding on the officer's lap. I assumed he wasn't fond of wearing a breakfast sandwich in that vicinity because he got quite angry.

While trying to wipe off the egg and cheese, he roared, "Get me that license and registration, now!" I complied. He looked at the registration and asked, "Your name Motorola?"

"No sir, it's a company car, not mine," I said.

"Speeding, assaulting an officer and operating a stolen vehicle," he responded. "Turn around and put your hands behind your back, sir."

There I was face down on the trunk of my car, handcuffed, having assaulted a police officer with an Egg McMuffin, the smell of hash browns wafting through the air, staring at the world's largest peanut at the Ashburn entrance ramp to I-75. Perhaps you have been in a similar situation?

On the way to the county jail, I tried several times to explain that the Egg McMuffin acted on its own and that it wasn't intentional assault, but he wasn't buying it.

When we arrived at the jail, I was put into a cell with the largest, tallest, most barefoot person I had ever seen.

He told me that he was in the hoosegow because he had, *"Twis'ed* a man's head off."

He asked me what I had done and I told him. "I assaulted an officer with an Egg McMuffin."

For a brief moment I thought I saw true fear in his eyes but decided he was just trying to figure out how an Egg McMuffin could be used as a weapon.

Dumbfounded, he started to ask, "How ken a Egg ..." but then stopped and just stared at me without blinking.

I asked to make a phone call to one of my sales representatives who lived close by but was not given the opportunity to use a phone. You can imagine how surprised I was when Tommy Rainey walked in and unlocked the jail door himself. He came into the cell laughing, walked right by me and shook Mr. "Man-ape-barefoot-twis-a-man's-head-off's" huge hand.

Tommy looked at me and said, "Got ya!" Suddenly the rest of my sales team materialized from around the corner, the officer who arrested me came in smiling (his lap still covered in Egg McMuffin) and Bigfoot, my cellmate, introduced himself as officer Roundtree.

By the way, I need to mention that all of the names in this book have been partially changed to protect the innocent, but mostly just to protect ... me!

Everyone got a big laugh out of this practical joke except me. It was a harrowing experience. It seemed impossible that I was actually being arrested, but it was a real cop in a real cop car, a real world's largest peanut, a real jail cell and a real Bigfoot. I found out Tommy was a part-time deputy sheriff and had orchestrated the whole ugly episode. So here I was, failing as a sales manager, not respected by my team, and now on top of everything else they were all having a huge laugh at my expense.

That night at dinner my team told me I was the worst and most useless boss they had ever had.

Their actual words were, "You are the worst and most useless boss that we have ever had!"

Out of desperation I managed to choke out a weak, "Why?"

Tommy's response was candid and honest. "You don't know how to manage people," he said. "You sold a lot of two-way radios up in Rome, but

"You Are Under Arrest for Assaulting an Officer with an Egg McMuffin®."

that doesn't mean you were a good sales representative and certainly doesn't make you a good sales manager. You took over and started telling us what to do without taking the time to get to know us or find out what we might need. But the worst part is you don't listen! When we come to you with a problem, you're more concerned about what you're going to say than you are with listening to the problem!"

He leaned in close and continued, "We had you arrested for two reasons. First of all it was really funny!"

Dave jumped in at this point and blurted out, "Especially when you were first put in the cell with Roundtree ..."

I managed to stop him by saying, "OK. I was there. Now what was the other reason?"

Tommy continued, "Second, we wanted to demonstrate that we can do anything we want to you." Tommy could tell his last comment had me a bit unnerved. So, he quickly said, "Calm down! I didn't mean it like that. What I meant to say was we can make you a hero or we can get you fired. We've been here a long time and we aren't going anywhere, but you might be."

Tommy went on to say, "If you want to be a good manager I'll tell you how. First of all you need to understand how we work with, sell to and service our government customers. That means you need to make sales calls with us, be quiet, listen and learn. Next, after you give us our sales quotas, we'll tell you if we can make them or not. If we can't, we need for you to go back to headquarters and try to negotiate lower ones. Once quotas are set, we'll tell you what tools and support we need from you. Again, you need to listen and then you need to go get what we need. After that, just stay out of our way unless we need you for something else. Follow these steps and we will make you a star. Oh, and every once in a while just say, "Thank You!"

As mentioned before these sales reps had been with Motorola for years and had been very, very successful. One of the four had been nominated for induction into Motorola's "Galvin Master" program, which was an exclusive fraternity of professional Motorola sales people named after the founder, Robert Galvin. Another wasn't far behind in being nominated and the other two also were very strong. They really didn't need me to teach them how to sell, and I already knew I didn't know much about managing people. But to hear them say, "Just stay out of the way unless we need you for something else!" was really degrading and embarrassing. How could I be the boss if they were telling me what to do?

The ride home the next day was very lonely and miserable. As I passed the world's largest peanut I slowed down to 45 and broke out in the "Waffle House sweats." I wasn't taking any chances. I stayed at that speed and kept a sharp eye for cops for the next couple of miles. I had been "sprung from the hoosegow" and planned to stay "sprung!"

I thought a lot about what the team had said the night before and realized they were right. I couldn't possibly help and support them unless I better understood how they sold and what they did to be so successful as sales people. As hard as it was to admit, I was adding no value and, in fact, I was simply in their way. I wanted to be a good sales manager, but it was obvious I wasn't off to a good start.

I decided the first step toward becoming a good manager was to learn how these salespeople became so successful. Only then could I learn what I needed to do as a manager to support them. Although I was still embarrassed and humiliated, I was smart enough to know I had four very good teachers around me. So, over the next six months I spent almost all of my time in the field riding and working with them. Morale improved, sales improved, and I was busy supporting them in every way.

I learned a great deal about these four excellent sales people while I was their manager, ahh ... I mean their assistant. How they sold was a very personal thing and all approached it differently. I learned, however, that in spite of these differences, they shared similar mindsets, practices and sales activities that characterized their success in sales. The most important thing I learned, though, was how to manage without getting arrested again.

I Always Knew You Were the Crazy One of My Boys!

Although happy at Motorola, I was presented with an opportunity several years later to join a tiny start-up company owned by AT&T called Advanced Mobile Phone Service (AMPS). This tiny company worked for many years trialing a concept known as cellular mobile telephone technology. The trials proved successful and the Federal Communications Commission (FCC) gave AMPS licenses to build cellular mobile telephone systems in a number of cities throughout the United States.

It appeared to be a risky job as there was a lot of debate and skepticism regarding how well the technology would be received. The telecommunications industry was abound with opinions, and experts were very outspoken!

"People driving around talking on the phone? It will be a high-priced fad. Are you outta your mind? I always knew you were the crazy one of my boys! Did you get fired from that good job you had at Motorola?" asked Mom.

I was hired by AMPS to build the sales organization in the southeast United States and was among the first group of employees in the southeast division. In essence, I was the sales department. We literally started from scratch. This was a brand new industry and we didn't have any models to work from, so I got busy developing and writing training courses and compensations plans, creating order forms and sales brochures, as well as interviewing and hiring sales people.

I taught the sales training classes myself; I taught the first one in Miami with 20 people attending. Every imaginable kind of sales representative was drawn to sell this exciting new technology. The training consisted of cellular system operation, mobile telephone product knowledge, pricing and how to overcome objections to an unproven technology.

At the end of the first day of training, I realized I had a problem. A huge disparity in experience and sales expertise existed in the class. It was obvious that the most inexperienced sales people would have a tough time trying to sell a new technology while still developing their own sales skills.

I pulled an "all-nighter" and put together a crash course called, "How the best-of-the-best sales people do it!" OK, the title is a bit unimaginative, but back then those "do it" bumper stickers were really popular. You know, the ones that proclaimed, "Scuba Divers do it under water!"

I found all my notes on what I learned from the best sales people I knew, managed and worked with at Motorola. I reviewed everything I observed and wrote down about all their similarities in mindset, practices and sales activities. I then grouped the information into like categories and created a formal presentation.

The process of organizing and developing a crash course confirmed several important things for me. First, working through the notes reinforced in my mind that although very successful salespeople come in all sizes, shapes and clothing styles, they have certain specific characteristics and practices in common. These common practices go beyond what they learned in sales skills training classes. Anyone can be taught sales skills such as handling objections (except maybe for me, considering my earlier account of handling Raymond Thacker's objections in the parking lot of the Cahutta Lodge near Ellijay, Ga.), but execution in some common areas appears the key.

Next, I realized and became confident I could organize, present and teach these characteristics and best practices to others. They could in turn use this knowledge to improve their own level of performance.

Finally, I learned that salespeople are hungry to know what the best salespeople do. The next morning in training class I announced I was going to present "How the best-of-the-best sales people say they do it!" Shortly after I began the presentation, everyone in the room scrambled for something to write on.

Why did they scramble for something to write on? Because the things that the best salespeople do to achieve great results are not always obvious! How each of us sells is a highly personal thing, and as such our approaches to the process and the customer are all a bit different. Since it's highly personal, it's difficult to simply observe the best salespeople and understand everything they do to achieve success.

Learning to sell is much like learning to play golf or tennis, studying music or art. We learn how, and over time we develop our own highly personal style. But some develop the ability, in their own highly personal way, to excel. We can all learn to play golf. There are, however, personal aspects specific to the best golfers. Their mindsets, improvement methods, habits and disciplines take them to the highest levels. That's what people want to learn from the best in a category. What if the past 10 Master's champions showed up at a golf club one day to talk about their games? I would dare say every avid golfer would scramble for something to write on.

As the company grew, we hired more sales representatives. I continued to learn from the best of them, and I also continued to teach what I was learning. As the sales director for the company, which had by then been renamed BellSouth Mobility, my goal was to learn more, better organize the information and then further develop the presentation. Over time, I made a science of my approach to learning, and I never missed an opportunity to learn more and compare what I learned to what I had already learned and collected.

At our company, like almost all others, we would honor the best performers quarterly and at the end of each year. I would generally ask specific individuals and excelling groups to tell me, in their own words, what they did to achieve and sustain their success. Sustaining success was the key. We all know the "one-hit wonders" who sold a year's supply of toilet paper to a hotel chain in January and made his or her quota for the entire year. I screened these people out and focused on those who had sustained performance.

I routinely made outside sales calls with the best salespeople at our company, spending a couple of days each week in the field. I spent time in the telesales centers listening to our best telesales representatives working with customers calling in or when they made outbound calls. I became a fixture on the sales floor in our retail stores shadowing the star performers. I watched and listened as they greeted customers, asked questions and matched products to their needs. I paid close attention as they made sales presentations, handled objections and demonstrated their closing skills and follow-up practices. Observation was one way to learn, but I followed up with each of them and asked why they thought they were successful. I compared what they said to what I observed.

I also developed a survey that contained open-ended questions. In the survey, I asked salespeople to tell me about the characteristics, practices, selling activities, expectations and motivations they felt made them successful. It was effective because people really had to think about what they did and how they did it before writing down an answer.

In addition, I often asked our customers what they felt the best salespeople had done or should do to ensure customer satisfaction. From time to time I would receive letters from customers commending a specific sales representative for having done a great job. I would call the customer to thank them and delve a little deeper to find out exactly what the sales representative did to exceed the customer's expectations.

I didn't limit my research to just our company or industry. I also asked top-performing salespeople who worked at other companies the same thing. Why are you successful? I would meet them at Chamber of Commerce meetings, networking clubs, industry conferences and other gatherings where I was either a speaker or participant. I met them when buying or selling a house, at department stores or automobile dealerships.

Yes, some excellent auto dealership salespeople exist. Perhaps not as many as in other professions, but some very good ones ply their trade. Or perhaps, since the car-buying experience is one during which we expect to be yanked around from the start, a good automobile sales representative yanks us around intentionally to ensure that our expectations are met. (OK, I realize this is a stretch, but I'm trying to give them the benefit of the doubt.)

I Always Knew You Were the Crazy One of My Boys!

I hate buying cars! I don't like the game.

I had a sales representative at a dealer once walk up and say, "She's a real beauty, don't you think? I can see you sittin' high and proud in that baby. Wanna test drive her?"

"No thanks," I said. "I've driven one like *her* before. I know how *she* will handle."

He responded, apparently not noticing I was making fun of his description of *her*, "Want a coke?"

"No thanks," I said.

"We have a really big sale going on and our sales manager told us today to bring him any offer," he pressed.

The car was about $30,000, and I wasn't planning to spend more than $25,000. "No thanks," I said. "It's way out of my price range."

He pushed some more. "Oh come on, make an offer. The manager is desperate; it's the end of the month. He said bring him any offer."

I wondered if he could be shooting me straight. Perhaps folks like Oprah and Dr. Phil were actually having an impact on the conscience of mankind. As a result of their syndicated talk show work, perhaps real estate salespeople have replaced those 20-year-old pictures of themselves on their business cards with current ones. Perhaps information technology (IT) people have dropped that "What did you do to it?" attitude when something goes wrong with your computer. Perhaps car salespeople have lost their "yank you around" demeanor that makes us all crazy.

Thinking maybe I could get a deal and that the boss was really desperate, I took the bait. "OK," I said. "How about $25,000?"

"Let's write her up!" he said. "Can I get you a coke?"

Everything was *her* to this guy. I sat patiently for 20 minutes while he wrote *her* up. Then he had me sign the offer and off he went to see the manager.

35

Ten minutes later he came back, sat down and said, "Well, the boss made a counter offer."

He handed me the offer I had signed for $25,000, which now had a counter offer of $29,500 on it. Somehow, despite the fact I was frustrated I had wasted 45 minutes of my time, he convinced me to make yet another counter offer of $26,000. Off he went again. This time he was gone for another 10 minutes.

I've always believed that car salespeople take offers into a special room where the counter offers are obtained within seven seconds. They then watch TV, play pool, tell jokes, smoke, drink and generally screw around for 10 to 15 minutes before returning to the customer with the counter offer that in reality took seven seconds to obtain.

When he came back (I swear I saw him putting a TV remote in his pocket as he rounded the corner), he proudly boasted, "The boss came down again and we now have him on the run." The counter-counter-counter offer was $29,250.

I left.

I found that many of the successful salespeople I talked to were not easily able to verbalize or write down the keys to their success. They told me a lot of the obvious stuff, but they weren't as specific as they could've been. For example, one may have offered that he or she was a good listener. I may at that point have asked, "Why is it important to listen?" A whole new level of the "who, what, when and where" of listening would emerge.

I also found that some of the best had never tried to explain and may not even have understood why they were so good. I met a guy in the Atlanta International Airport who was coming back from a sales recognition event in Orlando. He was proudly carrying a "Road Runner" trophy having been in the top10 percent nationally with his company selling industrial cleaning supplies. I asked him to tell me in his own words why he was so successful.

"I really like dealing with people, they like me and I'm good at building relationships with them," he said with conviction. "Plus I'm a good golfer and you can't succeed in sales without being a good golfer. That's pretty much it, soup to nuts!"

Using the same approach I had used so many times, I asked, "Why is being good at building relationships important?"

He looked puzzled. "You have to build a relationship with folks," he said. "You can't sell to them if you don't! You have to get to know them, their birthdays, their wives' and kids' names, their favorite golf courses. Once the relationship is there, the sales come naturally!"

I was concerned my flight was going to board soon, and I was lucky enough to upgrade to first class with frequent flyer points, so I wanted to get to the gate. (Actually, I still had 30 minutes before boarding, but I've always feared that if I'm not early, some "scumbag" will take my seat, I won't be able to get him to move, he'll admit it's mine but won't get up, we'll call each other names, I'll demand my god-given airline rights and then be ejected from the plane while my luggage stays on board. So I'm always early and in my seat.) I asked Bob if I could call him the following week.

On Monday I got a call from Bob confirming our scheduled phone call. He also indicated he had mailed me some information about his company and its product line of industrial cleaning supplies. When the package arrived it contained two sets of brochures with case studies and testimonials, two business cards and a letter from Bob saying that one set was for me and he would appreciate it if I would pass the other set to the company that provided our cleaning services. Bob called again, the day before our scheduled call, to confirm that the time was still good for me. It appeared Bob was successful for many reasons beyond simply "liking people and being a good golfer."

The Attributes and Practices of the Best

While working at Motorola, you may recall that I focused on becoming a good manager. OK, so focus was forced on me by a police officer and a jail cell, but it worked nonetheless. Once focused, I made it my mission to learn everything I could about the excellent salespeople who worked for me so I could better support their efforts. I took this assignment seriously and took detailed notes on their actions, sales practices, how they managed and organized their sales calls, what they said when they made cold calls and what I could do to help.

As time passed, other salespeople within Motorola joined my team, and I continued to work with them in the same manner. When a new sales representative joined the team, I would use what I learned to teach them how to sell like the successful salespeople on the team.

Recall that when I joined AMPS and was teaching that first cellular sales training class in Miami, I found it was filled with salespeople with very diverse levels of expertise. I knew a sales training "crash course" was in order, but given the varying levels of experience and the limited time I had, I wasn't sure what would be most effective.

I pulled out and reviewed all of the old notes from my Motorola days to see what I could share with the class that might be of help. While going through the notes, I tried to organize the practices of very good salespeople into similar categories to better present them to the class. I ended up with about five or six categories of similar practices and attributes and settled in on five for the presentation.

As time passed, I learned more and continued to teach what I was learning. I also continued to survey salespeople and spend time observing them at work. I continuously revised the categories as I learned more about the attributes and practices of the best. After many revisions, I settled on seven primary areas in which these attributes and practices could be categorized.

The Seven Attributes and Practices of the Top 10 Percent

- **Character**
- **Mindset**
- **Expectations**
- **Self Education**
- **Sales Actions**
- **Customer Experience**
- **Motivation**

Why seven attributes and practices? Why not five as I initially had or 10, which is a popular number? After all, 10 is a good number. It's one syllable, rolls right off of your tongue and sounds like an honest number. Plus, it's used a lot. Just pick up a magazine and you'll find lots of "10" articles.

The 10 most beautiful people of the year!
The 10 ugliest people of the year!
The 10 best plastic surgeons of the year!
The 10 ugliest who then became the 10 most beautiful!
The 10 ugliest plastic surgeons!

It even appears in the title of this book – *Top 10 Selling!*

So, you ask, "Why not make it easy on us and use that commonplace, widely accepted and ever-popular No. 10 instead of that uncomfortable and odd No. 7? Certainly 10 wouldn't be much of a stretch. After all there are already seven; couldn't you just create three more categories?"

Well, it all boiled down to seven – hundreds and hundreds of responses, hundreds and hundreds of observations, hundreds of surveys and many dozens of group meetings and it all came down to seven categories.

After doing the presentation several times and gathering, observing, learning and practicing on an ongoing basis, I closed myself in a conference room one afternoon. My goal was to better organize and categorize the information in my presentation. I sorted through the information I had gathered, old and new, and grouped responses into like groups.

If a salesperson described certain things she did to prospect for business, make sales calls and close sales, I called these sales actions. Sales actions were placed in a stack, in one corner of the conference room under a piece of paper on the wall with "sales actions" written on it. If a sales representative described what he did to ensure customer satisfaction or his initial approach to the customer, I called this the customer experience. I placed the customer experience stack in the center of the conference table.

After sorting, re-sorting, merging and expanding categories many times, I wound up with seven stacks.

I suppose I could've forced a few responses or observations into a category here or there and ended up with five. Or, I suppose I could've more-narrowly grouped some responses to create more categories. In the end, however, seven just made the most sense.

The Character of the Best Salespeople

Let's talk about what a successful sales representative looks like. We begin with character. Character by definition is the personality, the combination of qualities, features, attributes, traits and abilities that distinguish one person from another.

Characteristics and traits, in the context of this section, aren't specific to those that have led to success in sales. My goal was to learn about the character of the person in a broad and more general sense. The objective was to find out if there really is a specific personality or character that is better suited for sales.

In addition, it's not that we need to know what the character of a successful salesperson is like so we can mirror it and become successful too! An understanding of character is presented to provide an appreciation for the fact that success occurs in a variety of folks with a variety of characteristics. Also, it's presented to dispel a few myths about what makes a good salesperson.

We've all heard the stereotypical comments and jokes about salespeople, the traveling salesperson jokes, the used-car salesman analogies, the stories about the real estate salespeople not telling you everything, and how you can never find a salesperson after the sale. These can all be summed up into the oldie but goodie:

Question: How do you know if a salesman is lying?
Answer: His lips are moving!

Is it true that a really good salesperson can sell ice to an Eskimo? It's obvious that an Eskimo doesn't need to buy ice, but are we saying that a really good salesperson is one who can sell you something even if you don't need it? Is that what makes up the character of the best of the best?

Quite the contrary! Let's take a look at what the characteristics of the best salespeople look like. Following is a summary of the attributes and qualities that the best most often use to describe themselves, as well as what I've observed.

Character

- **Friendly**
- **Outgoing**
- **Determined**
- **Persistent**
- **Confident**
- **Independent**
- **Team member**
- **Passionate**
- **Honest**

Friendly

You don't have to be the "Most Likely to Succeed" in high school to become successful in sales. Being funny, outspoken and the "life of the party" might be what some successful salespeople are made of, but the vast majority aren't on stage all the time. Almost all of them are, however, friendly. That isn't to say loud, in-your-face friendly and run-the-show friendly, just friendly.

Outgoing

This doesn't mean "jumping around like Tom Cruise on Oprah's couch" kinda outgoing. Nor do you need to be the type who is the first to shake hands with everyone in a room full of strangers to be successful in sales.

The Character of the Best Salespeople

I was in the local bar and restaurant in the town where I live one Friday evening when two guys started wheeling in karaoke equipment. I watched as they set up the equipment while the most successful of the local real estate sales ladies flipped madly through the list of songs to find just the right one. When the karaoke hour struck she was the first person up on stage. Before the music even started, she was dancing and introducing herself to the audience. She did a pretty good job of singing *Sittin' On the Dock of the Bay* in spite of the sporadic, unwanted accompaniment from two other ladies, a drunken golfer and a diaper-clad toddler.

When the applause died down she thanked the audience and announced, "If any of you want to sell your house just give me a call. I'm also here most Friday nights."

As she took her place at the bar, the man next to me commented to his date, "That woman is a natural born salesperson. I could never get up in front of a crowd like that and talk, let alone sing."

The best salespeople do *not* describe themselves as karaoke stars or those who know how to "work a room." They describe themselves as sociable or responsive to others. They might not be the ones to initiate conversation, but they certainly would be responsive in return. Outgoing shouldn't be confused with simply being friendly, for there are degrees of friendliness that can be seen in outgoing people.

Determined

Without fail, every successful salesperson describes himself or herself as determined in all aspects of work and play. They say they were determined as children, students and adults. Descriptions such as firmness of purpose, firmly resolved toward achievement of goals, settled on objectives, decided in opinion or set in purpose were all commonly used phrases. In everything they undertake, business and personal, they establish goals, figure out what needs to be done to get what they want and then move forward with resolve.

Persistent

The best will tell you, however, that it takes more than determination to succeed. They will tell you they have watched some of the most determined around them fail. They will tell you it takes determination and persistence. Persistence is refusing to give up doing the things required to accomplish the goal. It's refusing to give up, even when working to reach a goal that seems unreachable.

When my oldest son was 13 he played little league baseball. He was a good outfielder, but when it was his turn to bat he couldn't seem to swing at the ball. His fate was solely in the hands of the pitcher. The pitcher would either walk him or strike him out while my son stood there with his bat firmly planted on his shoulder.

The coach would often ask my son why he couldn't seem to swing the bat, and my son would respond, "I'm gonna hit one, coach. I'm just waiting for the right pitch to hit."

One day, the coach pulled my son aside after the first pitch flew dead center over the plate without my son moving a muscle. "Son," he said. "You're not going to hit any of the ones that you don't swing at."

After this incident, my son swang the bat at almost every pitch no matter how good or bad it was. He had always been determined, but after the coach's words he changed his plan, became persistent and never stopped swinging. Unfortunately, he struck out a lot more because he swung at every pitch. Every once in a while he would connect with one, and when he did he would always knock it deep into left field!

Confident

We've all seen him. The guy with perfectly matched clothing, no wrinkles, no stains, hair perfectly in place, no zits, nothing between his teeth, in great shape, confident that he can do anything, become anything and do it all while looking great and without breaking a sweat. And his girlfriend, walking along with him in the mall, beautiful hair, perfect outfit, the body of an Olympic gymnast, recently accepted to Yale, confident that she can do it all too and that he's very lucky to be with her.

I don't like them!

Fortunately, this isn't what top salespeople mean when they describe themselves as confident. Otherwise, we would dislike them all – great looking, in great shape, nothing between their beautiful white teeth and great salespeople to boot.

What they mean when they speak of confidence relates more to feeling assured and free from doubt about their own abilities and skills, but not in an arrogant way. They believe strongly in themselves and their ability to accomplish what they set out to do. Many of them said they are the type to step up and take a leadership position when a leader is needed.

Stepping up to take charge for some reason always reminds me of a story about a friend of mine who took his 5-year-old daughter to church for the first time. He was a devout Catholic, so he knew all too well what went on just before the priest came out to say mass.

When the song leader started toward the microphone, my friend looked at his adorable little girl and asked her, "Would you like for me to get everyone to stand up and sing for you?

She looked at him with big wide eyes and a huge smile and said, "Yes!"

His timing was perfect, and just as the song leader leaned into the microphone, my friend stood and picked up his little girl. Seeing this, everyone else in the church also stood up and began singing.

He did have a bit of trouble for the rest of the service, however, as his daughter asked him repeatedly to get everyone up to sing the song from *Mr. Roger's Neighborhood*.

Independent

All successful salespeople state they are independent. Many will tell you they have always been that way. They were the ones in school who always turned in long-term projects on time. And you could tell that their long-term projects were actually done "long-term" instead of having been put together the night before. When given a project, assignment or job to do at work, they were able to complete it without having to be watched over by management. This doesn't mean they believe that they don't need to be managed. You'll find that the most successful salespeople are typically easily managed and that they value that management. In addition, it isn't that they don't want to be around other people. It simply means they can work alone successfully without the need to be in a normal workplace environment and without having continuous supervision. Not everyone can do that.

You may be saying to yourself about now, "I can work without continuous supervision. I would love to take my laptop, get out of this office and work from home or Starbucks."

Being able to work independently is not quite as easy as simply equipping yourself with a laptop and a Wi-Fi connection. There are a number of elements to consider. First of all, the best are able to work effectively without the need to physically be located in an office environment with support systems and co-workers close at hand. Many need the ability, throughout the course of the workday, to interact with others quickly and to do so face-to-face. Many need to be able to present issues to their boss, get feedback or help in real time and face-to-face.

The best are able to interact and coordinate remotely with co-workers and supervisors in very effective ways. We all probably agree that being in an office environment affords the ease of being able to simply go see someone who you might need. The best, however, are very efficient at coordinating with others by phone, fax and e-mail.

In addition, they are self-disciplined in terms of planning to accomplish their goals. They typically develop short- and long-term plans to achieve their sales objectives and self-manage toward achievement. They are pros at ruling out distractions when working in hotel rooms, a commandeered conference room or the dreaded "home" office.

When I first arrived in Rome, I decided to build an office in the spare bedroom of my home. There was a small, local Motorola sales office where I could have worked, but I thought it might be more efficient working where I lived.

If you haven't said it yourself you've most certainly heard it: "How great? I can get up and go to work in my pajamas! I'm sure I'll work more hours because there's no commute and I'll get more done since I won't have interruptions. Plus, I'll get to see the kids and dog throughout the day! It will be great!

The problems begin immediately for personality types like mine. I couldn't work unless the floor was clean. I would look up from my phone and see something on the carpet and the next thing you know I was vacuuming the rug. When you take a quick break in a normal office, you stop and talk to a few co-workers, but soon they have to go back to work. Since there's not much else to do in a normal office but work, you're soon back at your desk as well.

When you take a break at your "home" office, there's a lot you can do. You can replace that ugly chandelier in the entrance foyer, change the oil in the car, walk the dog 17 times or build a nuclear particle accelerator.

Just two weeks passed before I realized that my "home" office life had come to an end. I remember being in my "office," still in my jammies, unshaven, door locked, with a towel shoved under the door for soundproofing. I was whispering a price quotation and product proposal to a prospective customer so the kids wouldn't hear me and barge into the office. The good news was that the kids couldn't hear me. The bad news was that the customer couldn't either. He asked me to speak up, and I whispered that I couldn't because the kids would find me. He then asked me to meet him for lunch at the Waffle House in 20 or 30 minutes. Had I been shaved and in my suit, I might have been able to make it, but it's a law in most states, Georgia being one, that you can't shave and wear a suit to work in a "home" office. In other states, although not a law, it's just not done.

I whispered to him that I really needed an hour. He couldn't hear me and asked me to repeat what I said. I did so in a normal voice, and the cat was out of the bag. The kids attacked the door and the dog cut loose barking. The prospective customer then whispered back that we should plan to meet some other day, making some vague reference to something "freezing over," and he hung up.

It struck me as odd the first time I heard a telesales representative in a cubicle describe herself as independent. I've heard that from outside salespeople many times, but how independent can you be when you're working in a box surrounded by 500 other people working in boxes. Her job was selling home heating and air conditioning equipment service agreements. Throughout the course of quoting service agreement prices to customers, she had to routinely coordinate with service technicians, air conditioning manufacturers, builders and her supervisor. She had taken the initiative to develop her own vast library of resource information that contained builder contacts, technical specifications, manufacturer documents, model number cross-reference charts and up-to-date subcontractor pricing. She had done this on her own and was able to literally sell 30 percent more than her co-workers. She told me she planned to retire in two years and that she was accepting bids from co-workers for her library.

Team Member

It would appear to be contradictory that the best salespeople are independent, yet also team players, but it's true. I don't want to jump ahead, but it's important to note that the best salespeople have a strong belief in the products they sell and the company they sell them for. In most cases the best salespeople didn't end up working for the company they represent by chance. They're proud of what they do and realize the product, the customer support infrastructure and the company are all part of a successful team. They wanted to be a part of a successful team with great products and probably made specific choices throughout their careers to be in those environments.

In 1983 I was one of the sales representatives selected to work for AT&T's first unregulated company, American Bell. The company was created to sell AT&T's new line of large telephone systems and computers. American Bell was built for speed, built to compete in the unregulated telephone and computer sales environment against the big players of the time such as IBM and Compaq. The best salespeople at AT&T were selected in a year-long process. I was literally surrounded by AT&T's best, and the power and dynamics of the team could be felt throughout. We all realized we were part of something amazing and that our success depended on our approach to the market as a team.

Passionate

Passionate was used often by successful sales people to describe themselves. "I'm a very passionate person. If I believe in something, I get very passionate about it."

In terms of how that relates to work they say, "I'm passionate about what I sell" or "I'm passionate about the company I work for" and "I'm passionate about my industry."

Is it really passion they mean or is it just some of that crazy, dramatic, outgoing, karaoke, hyped-up-on-caffeine sales talk?

Enthusiasm is probably the best word to describe what they really mean. In fact, if you skip past the first two definitions in the dictionary related to love and then sex, the third definition of passionate is "boundless enthusiasm."

Honest

You already know I hate the process of buying a car. I love cars; I just hate buying one (or *her* I should say!). Years ago I was in a dealership and noticed that my sales representative had a bible on his desk. This struck me as a bit odd, as he had just finished cursing at a cloud in the sky (a golfer!) and condemning a vagrant fishing through a trash can on the edge of the car lot. Curious to know if he had learned any of those words from his bible, I asked him if he flipped through it during the day.

"Aahh hell no!" he said. "It's just a prop."

In a restaurant one evening I was handing my credit card to the server and noticed pictures of two cute kids in the inside cover of the plastic wallet that held the receipt. I asked her how old her kids were and she said, "Oh, I don't have kids. Those are pictures of Jill's kids." And she pointed toward another server close by.

We spoke earlier about the stereotypical view of salespeople in general. I think we can all agree that the sales profession is one that has its share of examples of less-than-desirable and unprofessional activities. And yes, in my opinion a server in a restaurant is in the sales profession.

With stories of high-pressure telemarketing sales representatives, CNN reports about scam artists preying on the elderly and the ever-present tales of used-car salesman, honest and good salespeople can sometimes be guilty simply by association.

Present in every response received from the best salespeople and throughout my observations of them, honesty was at the top of the list. Honesty in all regards, from pricing integrity, to product quality to features, benefits and setting performance expectations.

When I think of honesty, it reminds me of the early days building the sales organization at BellSouth Mobility in Atlanta. I interviewed a woman for a position in sales who said she was presently working as a *Soft Drink Spy*. The purpose of *Soft Drink Spy* job was to protect the renowned and trademarked name of a soft drink manufactured by a huge soft drink company.

She told me she would visit restaurants that had a reputation for serving customers a similar product made by a different soft drink company and *not* telling customers that it wasn't the real thing. She would order a drink, put a sample of the drink in a flask, put it in her purse, get a receipt and take the sample back to the company's lab. Test results and receipt in hand, she would go back to the restaurant and offer them an opportunity to begin carrying their product. If they declined the opportunity, she would get the legal department involved.

She said she loved the company and drank the soft drink, but she didn't like her job. She said it made her feel sneaky and that her purse was always sticky inside. She said the final straw came on Thanksgiving Day at her grandmother's house when she found herself attempting to take a sample of her iced tea to put in her purse.

It's not that her job was dishonest or placed her in a compromising position in any way; she felt a bit deceptive having an ulterior motive to simply ordering a drink. She's an example of extreme honesty in practice. I found, however, that her strong sense of honesty was mirrored in every one of the top 10 percent of sales professionals I interviewed, knew and worked with. By the way, she was our No. 1 salesperson during her first year.

The Mindset of the Very Best!

Mindset is defined as the fixed mental attitude or disposition that pre-determines a person's responses to and interpretations of situations. Mindset is different than *character,* which by definition is the personality, the combination of qualities, features, attributes, traits and abilities that distinguish one person from another.

Mindset is not who you are, but relates more to the habits that you have formed and developed from previous experience. For example, you might be a friendly person, which is related to your character. You might also be enthusiastic, which is defined as overflowing with a feeling of excitement, enjoyment or approval. Being enthusiastic about something, however, relates more to how you react to something based on previous experience. Enthusiasm therefore is a mindset developed from experience over time.

Let's now explore the mindset of the very best sales professional who I have known and worked with.

Mindset

- **Enthusiastic**
- **Self-motivated**
- **Belief in company and product**
- **Right the first time**
- **Avoid the negative, look for the positive**

- **Think like the customer**
- **Resilient**

Enthusiastic

The best salespeople are enthusiastic about selling. They're full of excitement and enjoyment about what they do for a living. They enjoy selling; they enjoy selling their product and enjoy working for their employer. Enthusasm was almost always the first description given by the best salespeople when talking about mindset.

One very enthusiastic salesperson once said, "If I was any more enthusiastic about what I do, I would have to charge my customers an entertainment tax when I made a sales call!"

The best developed their enthusiasm for selling over time through experience. Many will tell you they may not have always been filled with enthusiasm, but have become enthusiastic over time. They may not have originally been happy with what they were selling or who they were selling it for. They may have had a tough time learning how to sell when they started out.

I'm a classic example. Taking you back to my first sales call in the lumberjack camp high atop Pine Log Mountain in North Georgia, I wasn't enthusiastic. I was terrified! Now there's a mindset – terrified! That particular mindset, however, is not one you normally see in the top 10 percent of all salespeople. Over time I became enthusiastic based on more successful and pleasant sales experiences.

Self-motivated

If *independent* were to marry *self-motivated*, *self-motivated* would be the "better half." (What am I, 6 years old? What a stupid example!)

To motivate someone is to provide them with incentive to act in a certain way or do a certain thing. If the thing you want someone to do is perceived to be positive and if the steps aren't too complicated, then motivating them is easy.

"Here, eat this Snickers candy bar! It tastes good."

Now let's pretend you've never tasted a Snickers candy bar (far fetched I know, but work with me on this one) and you don't know if it tastes good or not. The incentive to act and eat the juicy Snickers bar is that we are told that it tastes good. There are three obvious steps to get to the act of it tasting good – grab it, unwrap it and put it in your mouth (as opposed to stepping on it or throwing it). From that point forward, self-motivation to eat a Snickers bar is easy.

Motivating oneself is a much more difficult task, however, if the benefit of the act to be undertaken isn't perceived to be positive or the steps aren't obvious. Even if it's known that the outcome will be positive, if the steps are complicated, it becomes difficult.

As I mentioned before, working from my "home" office was a disaster for me in the early days. I had no idea where to start in my new territory and didn't know what I was going to say if I made a cold call. As a result, I had trouble motivating myself to leave the house. I made a lot of telephone calls and the apartment was very clean, but I wasn't selling anything. In those early days I needed guidance to help me learn how to make cold calls and work a territory. Even though I knew what my quota was and how much money I would make if I made quota, I didn't know what the steps were to get there.

When I moved into the local sales office, I began learning from those around me. I asked a lot of questions and learned what to say when I made cold calls. I also had a sales representative who guided me to picture the goal that I wanted to accomplish and to then work backwards to understand and develop the steps to achieve that goal.

The best are self-motivated. They'll tell you that at first it's a conscious and step-wise process that must be learned. It becomes a mindset and second-nature as the sales process is mastered and goals are achieved.

Belief in the product and the company

I was in the Dallas-Ft. Worth International Airport waiting to board a flight when I noticed that the salesperson sitting next to me had a *Top Gun* luggage tag on his lap top bag. I asked him what he did, and he said he was a pharmaceutical sales representative. I asked about the *Top Gun* tag and he explained this was his second year as one of the top performing salespeople in the company.

I asked him if he liked what he did and he said, "Yes, I do. I make people feel better."

Now that's belief in your product!

In an interview with one top performer for a wireless phone company, he said, "I sell convenience, relief and joy. I sell the ability to hear a voice and know if a loved one is OK after a disaster, to hear joy in the voice of someone with great news, and provide comfort to those in despair."

The best believe in their product and the company they work for. They believe what they sell provides a necessary service, improves the quality of life, saves lives, protects people or provides assistance.

The best salespeople work for companies that believe the customer is of utmost importance. They see evidence of this in their company's product quality, customer service and warranty commitment. They see evidence of this in the quality of their own management, the tools and workplace quality, the support and training offered to them and the financial stability of the company.

The best listen to their customer's concerns carefully. In the case of a valid concern, they will carry it to management and help in any way they can to resolve the problem. They do, however, expect the problem to be fixed. If the problems don't get fixed or if the products they sell fall short time and again, the best will eventually look elsewhere for a company to believe in.

Right the first time

This is a practiced discipline and a commitment, not a statement. The mindset of the best is quite simply to do everything that needs to be done right away, and to make sure that it's done right, right away. They don't procrastinate, don't take short cuts and don't leave it to someone else to do.

They believe that doing what they're supposed to do is their job. Doing it right doesn't end when they finish their work, however. They believe it's also their job to follow up with all others who have an effect on the outcome.

We will talk more about follow up later in the book in a future category.

Avoid the negative, look for the positive

The best avoid the negative. They look for the positive aspects of everything in life. The best are the optimists. These people see the positive aspects of even the worst situations. More importantly, if they can't see positive aspects in a bad situation, they will work to find them. They will dwell on it, dig for it, rationalize it and find something good in every bad situation. They will walk away from those bad incidents having culled the positive from even the worst situation.

These are the people who make us all feel better when things look bad. These are the people who say, "Every dark cloud has a silver lining."

They avoid the folks who then say, "Yes, but thousands are struck by lighting from that dark cloud while looking for that silver lining."

The best are quick to say they avoid those who are consistently negative. They will tell you that you will often hear a great deal of negative all around you from salespeople who aren't doing well. And those who aren't doing well will often inappropriately blame the product, the pricing, company management or others for their lack of performance.

They are firm believers that you create your own success by focusing on the positive aspects but that sometimes you may have to go look for them. This can be especially true when related to knowing and selling the positive aspects of your product.

A sales representative, lets call her Sally, related a story to me that happened when she first started in sales. She was working for a very large international company that manufactured and sold telephone systems.

She was responsible for selling telephone systems to medium-sized medical offices. The primary product she sold was a very popular mid-tier telephone system. This system was a best seller for a number of years but recently was losing steam in the marketplace. There were many new competitive products emerging that were completely software-based, and almost all of them were cheaper than the one she sold.

Although her product had been upgraded and did incorporate a new software operating system, it still incorporated some older technology. It was termed a "hybrid" product. The term "hybrid" was a phrase coined by the company's product group responsible for the life cycle of this particular telephone system. The explanation of "hybrid" was that this was a viable product that made use of new software technology but still incorporated some older technology. This was a nice way of saying, "This is an older product but a good one, and it's highly profitable so keep selling it."

Sally hated to lose a sale, but she lost one when she proposed a new telephone system to a blood bank and was up against two competitors with systems that were entirely software-based. Her price was high and her competitors' technology wasn't "hybrid." One of her competitors won the sale.

She had lost the sale! She had even given blood!

Sally decided to find out what was good about her product. There must be something good about it, as it was still a part of the company's product line. She visited one of the design engineers at the manufacturing plant and asked him to tell her about the product. Sally said the conversation went kind of like this:

Sally: "Tell me about the system."

Engineer: "It's a hybrid."

Sally: "What does that really mean?"

Engineer: "It means it's older technology!"

Sally: "Why do we keep selling it?"

Engineer: "It's a good system, very profitable and we don't yet have an upgraded replacement for it."

The Mindset of the Very Best!

Sally: "Is it better than similar competitor's products?"

Engineer: "No."

Sally: "Does it have any features that competitive products don't have?"

Engineer: "No."

Sally: "Does it process calls faster?"

Engineer: "No."

Sally: "Is it more reliable?"

Engineer: "No."

Sally: "There must be something it does better than the competition?"

Engineer: "Well, there is one thing."

Sally: "What?"

Engineer: "It's easily expandable. It has a very, very powerful processor inside. Excessive if you ask me. Running at full capacity and doing self-diagnostics, it's only running at about 60 percent. It still has a lot of excess processing capacity."

Sally: "What does that mean?"

Engineer: "Well, you could expand the system to be twice its size with twice the number of telephone extensions connected to it without having to change out anything. With any of the competitor's comparable models you would have to buy a new one if you needed to grow it that big."

Sally: "Because of the very powerful processor inside?"

Engineer: "Yes, because of the processor inside. It is an *intel*® processor made by a company called Intel Corporation. (*intel*® is a registered trademark of the Intel corporation.)

(It is important to stop here and point out that this conversation took place long before the little *"intel® inside"* sticker began to show up on the outside of almost every computer.)

Sally: "It has an *intel* processor inside?"

Engineer "Yes, it has an *intel* processor inside.

Sally sold a lot of these "hybrid" systems based on what she learned that day. In all of the initial meetings with customers after that, she would ask if they expected to grow, and as you would expect almost all of them said yes. She would explain that her system was comprised of new, state-of-the-art software and time-tested architecture that was proven to be the most reliable. (In other words, a "hybrid.") She would also explain that the system could grow with the medical practice to twice its size without having to be changed out. And she probably said a thousand times, "All of this is because it has a very powerful *intel* processor inside."

Think like the customer

This is an old, old phrase. You will see it on the walls in call centers and in break rooms at retail stores. You will find it as a screen saver on desktops all around sales or service centers.

The best give the phrase life. They wrote paragraphs in my survey about what it really means to "think" like a customer. How does a customer think? First of all, it depends where the customer is in the sales process.

The best tell us they begin by reminding themselves that the customer probably doesn't know much about the product or what it can do for him or her. When you sell a product everyday, it can become easy to lose an appreciation for the fact that the customer is probably seeing it for the first time. Remember that the customer needs to start at the beginning while you might be trying to start at the middle.

For example, I was shopping for a laptop computer for my daughter for Christmas. I didn't know what she needed or what I should be looking for. A sales representative came up and asked if he could help. I said I needed a laptop. He pointed to one and said it was the most popular one right now and that there was a rebate on it.

I left and went to the another store down the road. I walked in and went to the laptops. A sales representative came up and asked if she could help me. She asked who the lap top was for, how she was going to use it, did she go to the Internet a lot and download music, etc. After about 30 questions she recommended one that wasn't the same as the one up the road. I bought it and asked her to fill out my survey.

The best salespeople start at the beginning with every sale. She told me she would naively approach every customer, ask questions and listen carefully. She said she asked questions so that she could truly understand what was needed and the customer would know they were getting what was needed.

This naive approach is a practiced art among the best salespeople. Mark, a very good sales rep who worked for BellSouth, told me, "I don't feel the need to demonstrate my vast knowledge of our product line to the customer. I check my ego at the start of the sale and listen like it's the first time I ever heard it"

Resilient

One very good sales representative in an outbound telesales center told me his single biggest strength was that he was resilient. A couple of days later he sent me the following:

From the American Heritage Dictionary of the English language
re·sil·ience [ri-**zil**-*yuh* ns, -**zil**-ee-*uh* ns]
    1. the power or ability to return to the original form, position, etc., after being bent, compressed, or stretched; elasticity.

"After making calls all day, this is the way that I feel," he said. "Bent, compressed and stretched. But I have the ability to recover quickly. I have to become enthusiastic again right after a series of bad calls or the next customer will hear it in my voice and I won't have a chance with them."

We talked about determination and persistence in the previous chapter. The best tell us it takes more than determination and persistence. It takes a resilient mindset. There are times when every sales representative will be bent, compressed and stretched. The ones who have learned to recover quickly have a huge advantage over all others.

One of the best sales representatives I ever worked with at BellSouth Mobility was also one of the most fearless cold callers of her time. She made more cold calls than anyone else to construction companies and sold more cellular phones than anyone else. After six months she made quite a name for herself, but one day she walked into my office and turned in her resignation.

"I just can't do it anymore," she said. "Ninety percent of the people I call tell me they have no interest. They're not mean and most aren't rude, but they still reject me and my product. I can't deal with being rejected all day long. It makes me feel bad and I'm sure people can sense it when I make that very next call."

Try as I might I couldn't talk her out of her decision. When I asked her what she was going to do, she said she was going back to school to become a nurse.

Expectations of the Very Best

Sales representatives have expectations? Who is working for whom here? Shouldn't it be the salesperson's employer who has the expectations? Perhaps the boss has expectations that the sales representatives will sell!

The best *do* have expectations. They're outspoken about what those expectations are and that they need to be fulfilled. It's important to remember that the top 10 percent make it happen. You've heard the adage, *Nothing happens until something is sold*. These are the ones who make it happen. They create sales, keep customers happy and buying more, and make their managers and the companies they represent successful. They can choose to do this for other managers or other companies if their expectations aren't met.

The best don't simply feel entitled, however. They aren't just sitting back waiting for all of their expectations to be fulfilled. They may be outspoken about what they expect, but they're willing to roll up their sleeves and help make it happen. They will surface problems, offer solutions, brainstorm alternatives and even commit to selling higher volumes if required to fix a problem.

So what do they expect?

Expectations

- **Good products**
- **Strong company**
- **Reward**
- **Recognition**
- **Sales opportunity**
- **Sales support**
- **Ongoing training**
- **Advancement**
- **To be a catalyst**
- **Quality management**

Good products

These people are the best. Chances are they didn't start out as the best; they had to learn how to achieve that status. Recall in earlier chapters that much of who they are they became over time. And as they improved, their expectations became clearer. If they were improving their ability to sell, but not selling a quality product, they would look for a quality product.

The best don't sell a thing so much as they provide a service; they fill a need, satisfy a desire or fix a problem. They listen well and work hard to understand what the customer needs and then work hard to ensure they pick the right product with the right features and appropriate options for the customer. Customers aren't really buying just a product from the best of all salespeople however. They're buying a solution, satisfying a desire or fulfilling a need based on the salesperson's recommendation. Imagine how the best salespeople must feel if the solution they've sold to a customer is compromised by a bad product.

Strong company

I was waiting to see a hospital administrator in Atlanta one day and was talking to a gentleman who also was waiting to see him. He worked for Hewlett-Packard selling medical equipment. He told me the administrator who we were both waiting to see was the reason he had gone to work for Hewlett-Packard. He said he used to be a sales representative for a company that didn't have the best reputation for quality and service. He knew his company's reputation wasn't the best, but he hoped over time that would change. In fact, he was successful at selling the products and felt he was making a difference himself, at least as it was related to service.

One day he was at the hospital making a sales call when he stopped by to say hello to the administrator. "When are you going to get a real job with a real company?" the administrator asked. "You've done a great job helping us figure out what we need, it's a shame you don't work for a quality company."

He suddenly realized he had seen little improvement in his company's products and couldn't overcome the reputation it had. He also saw nothing to indicate the company supported him in terms of improving its products and service reputation, so he decided to leave. He was determined to work for a strong and solid company. It took him a year and about 3,000 interviews, but he was finally hired by Hewlett-Packard.

The best say a strong company is one that has quality products and customer service, but that there's more to being strong. The company must be financially stable. This is important not simply because the salespeople want to get paid, but because the company needs resources to survive. If, for example, a company can't pay its vendors and subcontractors in a timely manner, they will choose to work with someone else. And they certainly will be vocal about not being paid on time.

In addition, the best want to work for a strong company with a leadership position in the marketplace. This doesn't necessarily mean the company has to be the dominant player with the largest share of the overall market. It does mean, however, that the company is the demonstrated leader in a niche market or is executing strategies to be so. Or, it could be that the company has only a small share of the market, but it's the highest-quality provider even at a higher price.

Finally, a strong company is one that has the marketing prowess to support the efforts of the sales organization and also the ability to respond quickly to competitive threats in the market.

Reward

The best salespeople are willing to take risks. If they aren't selling successfully, they won't earn much, but if successful they want the reward. They're confident they are the best and they can sell their product very well. They put in the hours, work hard and do whatever it takes to achieve both sales and income goals.

They expect the compensation plan to be understandable. In other words, they need to be able to quickly compute what they just earned as a sale is made. Outside factors beyond their control that affect their income aren't well received and prevent them from knowing what they just earned. As they make sales, they expect to see their progress toward attaining the stated sales goals. In addition, they expect the ability to easily see how they're progressing toward their income goal.

Most will tell you they are driven by money. They're also quick to tell you money isn't the only driver. They take great pride in how they represent their product and company. They also take pride in helping the company grow and gain a strong reputation.

Recognition

I had a boss at Motorola who was very strong on giving out awards at every sales meeting. As he got up in front of the room to begin handing out plaques to the top people, he would always take the opportunity to say, "I wish I could give all of you a raise, but if we can't pay you we'll plaque you." Silly as it sounds, those plaques were coveted and proudly placed on the winner's cubicle wall immediately.

The best expect recognition. They're driven by acknowledgment of their hard work and efforts. Sales meetings where successes are honored are very important to them. They're hard-working and independent and will tell you theirs can be a lonely job, especially when sales aren't going well. When things *are* going well, recognition is important, and even more important on those rare occasions when things aren't going so well. The best are still the best when things might not be going well, and these are the times when they need for management to remember that they're the best.

I always made it a habit at BellSouth Mobility to send a note to any sales representative who achieved his or her quota for the week. I bought hundreds of "thank you" cards and wrote a personal note to each sales representative thanking them for the hard work. I also included their percentage of quota attainment for the week and listed any specific, outstanding sales. I ended with a simple "Thank you!" When the sales force reached almost 300 people, I found myself spending most of my Mondays writing those notes.

At one point, I seriously considered raising quota to get out of writing so many notes. Kidding aside, I easily saw how well we were doing based on the number of notes I had to write. And I will say I *did* raise (and yes, sometimes lower) sales quotas as a result of the volume of notes I found myself writing.

Those notes meant more to people than I could have imagined. I often received calls and sometimes "thank you" notes saying how much they appreciated the fact that I took the time to recognize their work. And for years, when I was out in the field visiting sales offices, I would come across sales representatives who had kept a stack of them.

Sales Opportunity

The best advice I ever got on creating sales territories came from the president of a division of BellSouth Corporation.

He told me that the first step in creating territories is to imagine how many sales representatives you think you'll have in Georgia in 20 years – how many in outside sales, how many in telesales, how many in every sales channel from retail stores to major accounts. Then double that number for each channel.

He gave me an example. If your 20-year, doubled number is 1,000, divide Georgia into 1,000 different square grids. Then take the starting number of sales representatives that you have and give each of them one grid as their permanent territory. How many have you hired?

"Ten," I said.

"OK, then each of the 10 sales representatives gets one permanent territory and 99 temporary territories," he started explaining. "Let the sales representative help you pick which one will be their permanent territory, so you'll have buy-in. Then as you grow and add sales representatives, you can assign the territories being worked temporarily to the new sales representatives. Since the original 10 salespeople only had them to work temporarily, they won't feel like you've taken any opportunity away from them."

The method above may appear a bit extreme, but the point is valid. The best sales representatives will tell you they must have the appropriate amount of opportunity to make sales quotas and achieve their income goals. When you reduce their opportunity, they will react negatively because reducing opportunity reduces potential earnings. The best expect adequate opportunity and want assurances that they will have it.

Sales support

When I was a vice president and general manager at Cingular Wireless, I hired an account sales manager to take the lead in managing the Florida government account. He came from a competitor and was one of their top-producing account executives.

On his first day out of orientation, he stopped by my office and asked, "What kind of sales support infrastructure and systems can I expect?"

I remember thinking I needed to ask this guy to fill out a survey.

The best expect support. They are high-volume, high-revenue sales producers and they need and expect help to keep them in front of the customer and not wrapped up in paperwork.

Outside sales representatives expect to be wireless in every way with the ability to work remotely with a wireless phone, handheld PDA and wireless capability on their laptops. They expect customer relationship management (CRM) systems that allow for ease of entry of account sales, call information and order entry.

Retail sales representatives expect quality display areas, adequate inventory and point of sale systems that are quick and easy to operate.

Telesales centers sales representatives expect colorful break rooms! (Just kidding!) They expect efficient call-handling systems that allow them to handle calls and serve customers quickly. They expect to have the information they need online and at their fingertips to complete sales quickly.

All sales representatives expect sales support before, during and after the sale to allow them to move quickly to the next opportunity.

Ongoing training

I was wandering the mall waiting for my daughter and her friend to finish shopping and decided to look at the latest in plasma screen high definition televisions.

The sales representative's badge was covered in sales award pins that dated back a couple of years.

He asked me a lot of questions about where I was planning to put it, whether I had cable or satellite, if I was ready for HDTV, if I was planning to connect a surround sound system, etc. Then he led me down an isle toward the plasma wall. After passing through the graveyard of huge 35" tube televisions priced at $199, we got to the really big, expensive flat ones.

Why is it so loud in places where they sell big televisions? You literally can't hear your sales representative standing right beside you. In this case, the source of the volume problem, which could be heard up in the International Space Station, could be traced to three teen-age boys. Clad in jeans so low they didn't have to unzip them to go to the bathroom, wearing black t-shirts featuring their favorite bands and baseball caps on sideways, they were simulating a mosh pit and slamming into each other while viewing a *Green Day* video on a 60" SONY with surround sound.

I was suddenly captivated by this 60" marvel that displayed Billie Joe Armstrong's face as well as those of the other band member's 10 times the size of my own.

I screamed, "Wow, their faces are 10 times the size of mine. Tell me about that one."

"I don't know much about that one yet because it just came in," he screamed back.

We started reading about it on the display card that was recently placed in front of it. It was similar to the others in terms of size and specifications, etc. I noticed it had a lot of places to plug things into on the back *and* front. I don't have a lot of things to plug into it except a DVD player, but you never know when guests might stop by with video game machines that need to be plugged in.

As we learned about the 60" SONY together, my sales representative commented that keeping up with all of the new products could be tough. He said his company really needed to do a better job of training the sales team on where the new models fit in the lineup.

The best expect to be trained on their own products without having to learn through trial and error. They also expect to be kept informed about new product development news so they can better advise their customers on future products. It's also important to them to be updated about the products being offered by their competitors.

Finally, they expect to have ongoing sales training and job development training as needed to enhance their future growth within their company.

Advancement

Growing within a company is very important to the best salespeople. Advancement doesn't always mean sales management. The best want to advance to senior sales positions, become account executives or account managers. They want more responsibility, larger accounts and more lucrative territories. They want the responsibility of handling specific industry segments or working with the largest accounts. In short, they want to make larger contributions.

Many but not all of the best salespeople *do* want to be promoted to sales management. They want to be trained in management skills and then be given the opportunity to accomplish the larger goals of a team. It's important to them to be made aware of upcoming promotional opportunities and to then interview for the positions. If they're not selected, they want the courtesy of being advised of such before the chosen candidate is announced. Lastly, they want to be told where they fell short or what additional experience is required to improve their chances next time.

To be a catalyst

The best salespeople view their positions as the most important and critical jobs within the company. They're the eyes and ears of the company related to customers and often catalysts for change. Almost everyone in a company would say the same, but the very best salespeople have a very strong case for making this claim.

Let's look at an example from the world of automobile sales. Assume that the economy is suddenly taking a sharp downturn, gas prices are high and interest rates are climbing. You're an automobile manufacturer specializing in SUVs and trucks. Your models aren't as fuel efficient, comfortable, or feature rich and sexy items as some of the smaller sedans and crossover vehicles being manufactured.

In the past your vehicles practically sold themselves. Your dealer's salespeople didn't have to work too hard, weren't well-trained and were there primarily to write up the orders. The sales compensation plan was low. Needless to say, you didn't attract the best salespeople.

As a result of the economy, gas prices and interest rates, your salespeople are now having a tough time convincing your shoppers to buy your vehicles. They have a lot of opportunities, but they can't handle objections regarding fuel economy, comfort and sexy features such as trim and spoilers.

Sales drop, and it starts to effect production. The plant begins to lay off workers. Soon, the service department work begins to decline and mechanics are laid off too. Dealerships close and soon the company is acquired by the manufacturer of smaller, more fuel-efficient vehicles.

I blame it all on the salespeople. It was their responsibility to ask questions and handle objections in order to best sell their products. If the objections couldn't be overcome for valid reasons, they should have taken these concerns to top management and demanded change.

Your salespeople are the front line with your existing and prospective customers. For eight hours a day, five days a week and 50 weeks a year, these salespeople are listening to, talking with and negotiating with your potential customers. These potential customers are the people who will buy your products and give all other employees in your company jobs to do.

If you have no competition, the economy is strong and sell a great product that literally sells itself, you don't have a problem and perhaps don't care to hear what potential customers have to say. If, however, the prospective customers are comparing your products to competitors, have issues with your pricing, questions about your products features and concerns about your quality, you need to know it and *may* need to do something about it.

That's where the best salespeople come in. They accept that they're responsible for listening to prospective and existing customers and then championing their concerns to management. The best accept this responsibility and view themselves as the conduit between the customer and management. In addition, they expect action to be taken based on the feedback they provide. They consider themselves the catalysts to help produce better products and services.

Quality management

The top 10 percent of salespeople know they need good managers in order to ensure their own success. The best will seek out good managers to work for and work hard for them in return. Good salespeople know exactly what they expect from a good manager, and they aren't the least bit shy about telling them. To manage the best salespeople requires tough skin and endless energy. The manager must have an understanding of how the best sell and what support is expected of them.

The best tell us they have certain expectations of their managers, including:

Be available. This doesn't mean the manager must answer his phone at 3 a.m., but he or she needs to have voice mail, e-mail, a Blackberry, etc. and respond as soon as is reasonably possible.

Be a champion. The best salespeople expect their managers will do whatever it takes to get them the tools they need to do their jobs. In addition, they expect their managers to support them on issues related to product development and pricing issues resulting from competitive forces in the marketplace.

Be a mentor. The best require their manager to be a counselor, a teacher and a trusted friend.

Sometimes, simply be the boss. The best salespeople challenge upward often to voice their concerns and those of their customers. They acknowledge, however, that they may not always see the big picture, and there are times when the boss simply needs to give informed and knowledgeable feedback.

Be respectful. The best demand respect. The manager of the best salespeople knows they work endlessly to get the job done and achieve their sales goals. While they may need to be managed and guided from time to time, disrespectful tactics (I'm thinking of McDonald's applications here!) aren't well received and will typically draw harsh criticism.

Say thank you! Just stop by and say "thanks" once in a while.

Be fair and impartial. Management is expected to be fair in all regards related to ensuring sales opportunity. This means they must create equity as it relates to territory size, module opportunity and account value.

Listen to understand. The best salespeople expect their managers to be good listeners. They expect they will listen in order to understand, not simply wait for their turn to talk.

Listening reminds me of a lesson my daughter taught me.

Unfortunately, her mother and I were going through a divorce. She was just entering her teens and was having a really tough time with it. One night she had a meltdown. I was there and was "the target."

I'm not sure if any of you have been "the target" of a teen-age daughter meltdown, but you have a better chance of surviving as a guest on Dr Phil and hearing him say to you in front of three million people on national television, "You seem perfectly sane to me, and your kids are lucky to have you as a dad."

She caught me in the hall while charging to her room, and I was helplessly caught in the flow, being pushed, pulled and drawn into her room. I felt like I was caught by one of those tractor beams in *Star Trek*.

"We just can't help ourselves, Captain. The engine is at full power, but their tractor beam is just too strong."

I found myself sitting on her bed dumbfounded, unable to get a word in edgewise, listening as she blamed me for everything that had gone wrong in her life for the last 13 years. I knew the divorce was the real problem, but I didn't know what to say to fix it. I sat there and listened as she cried and yelled, not understanding half of what she was saying.

After spending a week in her room during the next hour, she suddenly stopped crying, sat up and said, "Thanks Dad, you really helped me."

"I didn't do anything but listen, princess," I replied.

"Sometimes all you have to do to help is just listen," she said.

Self-Education Practices of the Very Best

The best salespeople are always looking for opportunities to improve, grow and learn. They're the first to enroll in scheduled classes whether required or optional. They look for self-improvement opportunities both inside and outside of the company. They're always learning from the successful people around them. They will read about successful people, attend seminars, read their columns and practice what other successful people preach. In this chapter we will explore what the best tell us about their own self-education practices.

Self-education

- **Selling skills**
- **Industry trends**
- **Customer relationship management (CRM) tools**
- **Compensation system**
- **Product knowledge and product development**
- **Management training**
- **Continuing education**

Selling Skills

When the best talk about sales skills development they don't mean taking the same classes on selling over and over again. They're the first to acknowledge that refresher courses are very useful, as sales skills development is an ongoing education, but they also take this to a much higher level.

The best immerse themselves in reading everything they can find on selling, negotiating and customer relationships. They're always on the lookout for articles and columns in magazine and newspapers, online newsletters and the latest in books by the sales experts.

Those involved in government or large business selling, where sealed bids and requests for proposals are the norm, fully understand the Federal Antitrust Laws and stay abreast of changes.

The top salespeople constantly search for the latest in organizational and time-management tools and courses to better organize their workload and improve efficiency. They understand and use customer relationship management (CRM) software even if they have to buy it themselves.

If a workshop or seminar is being held locally by a renowned sales expert, the best will be the first to ask if they can attend. They see it as their responsibility to continue to grow and seek out opportunities to learn from the legends in sales and negotiating.

Industry trends

The difference between success in sales and marginal performance relates to how well a salesperson can relate to his or her prospect's needs. If, for example, you're a sales representative in the healthcare industry, ongoing education in the trends affecting the industry is essential to success. How can you know if your products can provide a solution without a full understanding of the trends, issues and needs of that industry?

As with sales skills education, the best constantly pursue ongoing educational opportunities within the industries to which they market their products. They will subscribe to their customer's magazines, attend their industry conferences and join any and all related associations as a supplier member.

You'll remember Tommy Rainey, the Motorola government sales representative who had me arrested. Tommy sold to the government market for almost his entire career at Motorola. His accounts were in public safety, police, fire and rescue. He read their magazines, attended their conferences, was a member of their associations and even became a part-time deputy sheriff. Tommy knew more about trends and issues in public safety than many of his customers.

Tommy was a huge asset to his customers and to Motorola because of his knowledge and involvement in the public safety industry. His customers viewed him as an expert in communications equipment and public safety. They trusted him and relied on his expertise to recommend products they needed. I'm quite certain that few – if any – Motorola public-safety products rolled off the assembly line without being reviewed by Tommy and other great salespeople like him.

Customer relationship management (CRM) tools

I mentioned CRM software earlier, but this valuable tool bears more discussion. The general sales population has not yet embraced the use of CRM tools fully. In conversations with salespeople, I discovered they don't see the value in the CRM systems they have at their disposal. They say they're being asked to input a great deal of information that does little to benefit them.

The average salesperson feels the company gets a great deal out of the database being created, but the information does little to improve their own efficiency. In spite of the fact that their companies have spent a great deal of money on these outstanding tools, many average salespeople simply input the minimum required to get paid their commission.

However, excellent salespeople will tell you they must keep great records. And to keep great records, they need great tools. The best salespeople embrace their companies' CRM systems. They take the initiative to learn about them and use the reporting abilities, account planning capabilities and forecasting tools. You'll find they input information immediately, completely and understand that the quality of their input increases the value of the tool.

Compensation system

Every year we would hold a sales meeting in early December to announce changes in the compensation plan for the upcoming year. During the break, the best salespeople would stay in their seats, pull out their calculators and figure out how they would attain their income goals for the next year. Then they would all meet in the back of the room to compare notes.

You'll never hear a top 10 percent sales performer say, "I didn't know that was going to happen!" related to the commission they received for a product. You'll find the best immediately educate themselves on a new compensation plan or changes to an existing one and that there are no surprises to them.

Every company designs and builds its compensation plan to accomplish specific goals. Their plans are designed to ensure that the sales force sells a specific mix of products with specific features and options at specific prices. If that formula is followed by a sales representative, he or she will maximize earnings under the plan. The best salespeople figure this out right away and sell exactly the way the plan is designed.

Product knowledge and product development

I would often hear from customers that their single biggest complaint about salespeople was they didn't know their product – the features, the capability or pricing.

The best take gaining an understanding of the products they sell very seriously. These people tell me they actually read the information that comes with the new product announcements instead of just looking at the pictures. Almost all of them say they make a list of questions that weren't answered in the material and start searching for answers.

They know lack of product knowledge is the single biggest complaint of customers everywhere, and they make it their goal to know everything they can about their products. They also learn as much as they can about their competitor's products. They're quick to tell you, however, that they never sell against competition by talking about their products much less by disparaging them. They always sell the strengths of their own products matched to the needs of their customers.

The best also spend a great deal of time learning about new developments on the horizon and how these will affect what they presently sell. I remember being pulled aside often in the hallway by our best salespeople who would ask me to tell them about a product under development that they read about on the Internet somewhere. Nine times out of 10 I was caught by surprise.

I talked earlier about the fact that the best consider it their responsibility to recommend change where they feel that change is needed. When it comes to product development, they view themselves as catalysts for positive change. They work everyday on the front lines where the true worth and value of a product meets the road. Customers are quick to tell them if their product falls short. The best are also quick to realize whether the product provides the solution to identified needs.

Often in meetings, while making sales calls or on the floor of a retail store, I was confronted with product development suggestions. The best were quick to point out they were hearing from customers that the new *Z-500 Turbo Blast Side Smacker* is wonderful, but it needs better battery life and more memory and needs to be fixed right away. Having built and managed BellSouth's wireless product development center, I knew a bit about product development and profitability lifecycles, so I know the chances of getting product changes done quickly are slim. What I *also* know is that these salespeople are our best opportunity to know what our products need to be, as they deal with our customers every day. And they make it a personal responsibility to tell us what our customers need.

While running the wireless product development center, I learned that almost every product we developed in a conference room, based on what we thought the customers needed, failed. Conversely, almost every product developed based on conversations, feedback and interviews with customers was successful. The best are listening all day long and giving valuable feedback. They expect to be listened to and for action to be taken as a result.

Management training

In the chapter on expectations, we talked about the fact that the best expect to be given opportunities for advancement. They don't, however, sit back and wait for development and training to be spoon fed to them. The best want to be ready when an opportunity presents itself.

Whether it's people management training or account management training, the best salespeople have mapped out their own education plan. Some of the plan includes courses taught within the company, while others are offered outside of the company.

Continuing education

Most of the best salespeople enroll in or plan to be enrolled in continuing education outside of the company. They're goal-oriented, self-development-minded people who want to accomplish their goals in life and see ongoing education as the key.

Whether they're taking undergraduate courses at a community college, online or getting an MBA, they're continuing to avail themselves of opportunities. You'll find that tuition reimbursement programs at the companies they work for are well utilized, if available.

Sales Actions of the Very Best Salespeople

The best do very specific things in very disciplined fashion each and every day to make sales happen. You can be the best salesperson, and the most knowledgeable about your products and your industry, but if you spend your day sitting in a bean bag chair watching *Wheel of Fortune* eating cheese crunchies, you'll sell very little. Granted, you don't have bean bags in the break room of a retail store or a telesales call center, but there are still a thousand things that can distract a salesperson from selling.

Not so with the best. They know what needs to be done, and almost all of them provide the same answers. They go beyond simply telling us what they do in their responses, however. They tell us how they do it and how they do it consistently.

Take the top 10 percent sales representative who worked for a business service company. The company she worked for provided small individual offices, answering services, administrative services and conference rooms for small businesspeople who couldn't afford a full-service office and staff. She told me she had her own business cards printed because the company didn't provide cards for the inside sales employees who worked in the center. Her job was to greet walk-in prospects who visited the center and tell them about the available services. Her hours were from 10 a.m. to 6 p.m. As often as she could, before starting work, she would make it a point to visit local copying and printing companies, chambers of commerce and office supply stores. She would tell them about her company and give them a stack of her business cards. The vast majority of the walk-in prospective customers asked for her by name when they came in. She was the top sales representative in the entire company.

Sales Actions

- **Be there**
- **Dress respectfully**
- **Prospecting**
- **Community involvement**
- **Work hard, yet balance**
- **Set measurable goals and continuously stay focused**
- **Closing skills**
- **Follow up on everything**

Be there

Dr. Michael Mescon is the Dean Emeritus of the College of Business at Georgia State University. In his book titled *Showing Up For Work*, he tells about a young student who after nine years of college came to him and said, "I'm ready to graduate. I want to be successful. I need your advice."

To which Dr. Mescon replied, "In that case, I will advise you … Show up."

The stunned student asked, "That is all the advice you have? Do you mean after nine years of paying tuition, attending classes, passing exams and studying, you're saying all I have to do to succeed is to show up?

Dr Mescon replied, "Well, that's actually the truth only about 70 percent of the time. That's because generally only 70 percent of people show up as they should. But if you want to increase your odds of success, show up, on time. And if you want to devastate virtually all competition, show up, on time, dressed to play! You won't even have to break a sweat."

It has been my experience that only about 80 percent of expected folks actually show up for scheduled business events. Of that 80 percent only 75 percent of them are on time. And of the ones who show up and are on time, only 65 percent of them are prepared and ready to do the work. In other words, if 100 people are expected at a business or training event, only 39 of them will show up, on time, prepared, having done their pre-work and ready to work.

Are these statistics any different for salespeople when they're going to scheduled appointments? The answer, in my experience, is no! The average salesperson mirrors those statistics; only 39 out of 100 are on time with their acts together and ready to answer a client's questions.

The best salespeople tell us they're there when they're supposed to be and ready to work. This puts them ahead of more than half of their competitors and almost guarantees their success.

Oh, by the way, did you know that 62.78 percent of all statistics are made up?

Being there in outside sales doesn't mean you need to be in the office at 8 a.m. every day without fail. When I was in outside sales, my job depended on making face-to-face sales calls. The hard part about the job was getting started each day. At first I went to the office at 8 a.m. every day. Many of those days I stayed there for the entire day. There was always something to do. On the days I did break away and leave, I seldom put in a full day of making sales calls.

You know what it's like. You stop by the office first thing in the morning just to get organized and return a few phone calls. You get coffee a couple of times, talk about last night's *American Idol*, and the next thing you know it's mid morning. You make a few more calls and are getting ready to leave when someone stops you to talk about Fantasy Football. Soon it's lunch time. You decide to have lunch and make sales calls in the afternoon. You get back from lunch and return a few more calls with the best of intentions of leaving soon. You get the "afternoon sleepies," need more coffee, and the next thing you know it's 4 p.m. It's now too late to make sales calls, so you pledge to make calls the next morning and head for home.

I learned quickly not to go to the office. My goal was to make 20 outside face-to-face calls every day. My promise to myself was to be in the field ready to work at 8 a.m. I started each day at a Waffle House somewhere in my sales territory at this time. I arrived, sat at the counter, got a cup of coffee and organized where I was going to make calls that day. You can only watch the cook make eggs and bacon at the Waffle House for so long, so by 8:30 I was in my car.

I love Waffle House. They greet you so nicely when you walk in. They also know my name in every Waffle House in the United States. Of course, it's my Waffle House name – Darlin'.

I remember going into my usual Waffle House one morning and being greeted by a new waitress who said, "Mornin' Sugar!"

Wilma, the regular waitress, came out from the back screaming, "That ain't Sugar, he's Darlin!" Then she said to the new girl, "Now listen sweetie, you are gonna need to learn to remember everyone's name."

In retail your Waffle House is the front door at opening time. The best say that *being there* in a retail store means being at the front door to open it and greet each customer as they walk in.

One retail sales representative told me, "There's a real good chance the guy waiting outside the door for you to open, occasionally knocking impatiently, isn't going to come in and say, 'Oh! I just came in to browse.' The first at the door are on a mission and want to get in, buy and get out. Those are your best closing opportunities."

How can you *be there* in a telesales call center? In a telesales call center aren't you already there sitting at your desk, ready for the calls to start coming in?

One of the best salespeople in a telesales center told me her secret was to be at her desk ready to log in and take calls before the center opened for business. "As soon as the calls start to come in, my goal is to be on line answering them," she said. "Many sales reps are still getting their coffee or getting organized, but not me. I learned a long time ago that it's easier to close the sales on the first calls of the day. Chances are good these customers made a decision last night, and they want to place an order and move on with their days. If the first call turns out to be a complaint, I handle it with the best customer care and sometimes those become my next sales opportunity.

Dress respectfully

I always wore a suit and tie when making sales calls. In North Georgia calling on lumberjacks and down in South Georgia calling on police departments, I always wore a suit and tie. I even dressed that way in South Florida where you see sales representatives in short-sleeved shirts and khakis. Many wore a tie, but not necessarily a suit, and some didn't wear either, but perhaps this was a contributing factor to my success.

One of my sales representatives in Miami once said to me, "Dan, lose the coat and tie. Construction customers don't trust a sales representative in a suit. They're hard-working, blue-collar people who don't need anyone dressing up and trying to impress them."

I always thought it was ironic he was wearing a $120 golf shirt.

I asked if he knew what a lumberjack was. He said yes. I told him I always wore a suit and tie when I called on them and they trusted me. He stood there and looked at me like the kid taking orders in a fast-food restaurant does when you ask for something difficult like a No. 5 with no onions.

He stared at me and eventually said, "I don't understand your point?"

He wasn't in the top 10 percent of the national sales force, by the way.

My father told me when I started in sales to always dress in a suit and tie. He said people want to buy from someone who appears to be successful. And he was right! People *do* want to buy from someone who is successful. Just ask yourself, when was the last time you went to a car dealership, walked up to the manager and said, "Can I talk to the worst sales representative you have?" My father also said that dressing well represents a sign of respect for your customers.

Now don't get me wrong, I'm not saying you have to wear a suit and tie to be successful. I *am* saying that it worked for me, though. It was and still is my work uniform. I've interviewed hundreds of very successful salespeople. Many wore suits and ties while many did not. In retail stores or telesales call centers a suit and tie isn't the usual dress. I will tell you, however, that all of the top 10 percent salespeople who I've known dressed for respect. Yes, even in telesales call centers whether they knew I was visiting them that day or not.

Prospecting

I was at work one Monday morning and it wasn't one of my best days. I was behind on about 208 projects, deluged with e-mail and getting ready for a three-day business trip. The phone rang. I answered it. It was a salesperson.

He said, and this is an exact quote except that I changed the name of the salesperson and the company, "Hi Dan, my name is Bob Smith with Efficiency Products and I want to buy you lunch and share my product with you. Can I come by and pick you up today?"

I said, "I'm busier than hell all the time and almost always eat lunch at my desk just trying to get caught up. I don't know you and can't imagine anything more miserable than to be trapped with you in your car and then be forced to sit across the table from you and try to eat while you pound on me to buy your product. All the while I'll be worrying about how much I have to do. Plus, I don't even know what your product is? Sounds like loads of fun for me Bobby!"

Ok, I said that in my mind!

What I really said was, "Today is not the best day, but can you tell me a bit about your product?"

"I share a product that will benefit your customer service people in terms of improved efficiency," he said. "Is tomorrow a better day for lunch?"

"Actually I don't handle the customer service centers, but I'll be glad to give you the name of the right person to talk with," I said.

What a horrible job of prospecting for business. Had I said "yes" to lunch, this guy would have spent the better part of his day with me only to find I wasn't who he needed to talk to. It would have been a waste to his company in terms of what they pay him and the cost of lunch, but take a look at the wasted opportunity cost for him. Had I not pushed back he would have wasted his time with me when he could have spent it with a real prospect. If he did just a little qualifying, even by asking me a few questions, he would have spent his time well.

And what was with that "sharing" thing. He was a salesperson. Sales people sell, they don't share. My thoughts go back to the character trait "honesty." Although Bobby wasn't being dishonest, he was attempting to cloak his true motive, which was to sell me his products.

The best are always prospecting for business. They've learned how to prospect and qualify to make the best use of their time as well as the prospective customer's time. They prospect everywhere – at work, home, in the neighborhood, at parties, church (OK, not at church, but out in the parking lot. No one will ever admit that one!).

They're constantly digging through newspapers looking for folks who have been promoted or moved to other companies. They're on the Internet searching for their target customers in the electronic Yellow Pages. You'll see them passing out business cards at chamber of commerce meetings, Rotary Club, Toastmaster's or Kiwanis.

The best join networking organizations like Business Networking International (BNI) or Breakfast Club of America. They join the serious networking groups – the ones that meet once a week and have a structured program for finding and passing qualified referrals, not just leads, to other members.

Referrals are the single biggest source of new business for top salespeople. They provide the best follow-up, after sales support and customer care, and their satisfied customers give them referrals for new business. The best aren't shy about it either. They ask for referrals at every opportunity.

And the best will tell you there are two things that make a difference in whether your customers will provide you with the names of their friends and co-workers. First, they have to know someone who needs what you sell. They know a lot of people – the lady at the bank, their doctor, 600 people they work with, the bowling team and their poker buddies. The best say that when you simply ask a customer if they know someone who needs what you sell, everyone pops into their minds. You have to help the customer narrow things a bit to get the best leads.

You might say, "Bob I know you're a member of the Nashville Chamber of Commerce. Do you know of anyone there who might need my products?" Now the customer is thinking of a population of fewer people and more than likely your target.

Second, you have to do good job and build a good relationship with your customer to even consider asking for a referral. The best tell us that a good relationship with a customer isn't about becoming his best friend, playing golf with him or knowing his kids' names so much as it's about "having done the right things the right way!"

Don't you hate those bad, yet unaware, sales representatives?

"Thanks fer shoppin' at Barbeque World. I'm sure that you are gonna love yer new Cow Cooker 2000 gas grill. Sorry I ignored you when you first came in and I was doin' lottery scratch-offs and sorry that I caught your hair on fire during the demonstration. Whodda thought them plastic steaks woudda caught on fire and splodded into air like that? Should grow back OK though! Anyhoo, yur gonna get a survey in the mail to fill out on me. You know one through 10 kinda stuff. Iffin you don't rate me all 10's I ain't gonna get no paycheck and the county's gonna take away my kids so I preciate your rating me all 10's. Well, that 13-year-old has been giving me lots of trouble! Naw, I wanna keep her too. So, go ahead and give me all 10's. Thanks again and ken you give me the names of your parents and neighbors on both sides so I ken call em up to come in and buy a grill from me?"

Whether prospecting for new business at a chamber of commerce event, calling a referral passed to you from an existing customer or browsing the Internet, the best tell us that qualifying the prospect is essential.

OK, so they prospect all the time. But they qualify all the time too. The best say qualifying is essential to prevent from wasting your time *and* the prospect's time. How do they qualify? They qualify by gathering as much information as they can in advance of that first contact. Can this individual or business utilize what I sell? Can they benefit from my service? Do they appear to have a need? Are they using similar products already? If this is a business, who should I talk to? Can they afford my products?

Community involvement

Almost all top 10 percent salespeople are involved in their communities. They coach sports, they volunteer at local community events and they're involved with fund raising groups of all kinds. You'll see them serving dinners at homeless shelters, at Boy's & Girl's clubs, volunteering at church events and as tutors teaching adults to read. Simply stated, "giving back."

When I ask why, most were quick to say it was their responsibility. They were blessed and it was their responsibility to give back to the community that had been good to them. Others said they got a lot out of helping others. Some admitted they originally got involved in the community for selfish reasons – to prospect for business or because an existing customer asked them to.

A top salesperson in Jacksonville once told me, "It seemed a logical way to meet people and network for new business. And I saw other top salespeople doing it and figured they must be on to something. So, I have to admit that my motives were initially strictly business-oriented. After a while, I realized I continued to volunteer at community events because I wanted to. I got a lot out of it. Not much business, but a lot of self-satisfaction and pride."

Work hard, yet balance

When my daughter was little I would read the Berenstain Bears to her every night before bed, and I also woke her up every morning. I remember one night working late and not getting home until she was asleep. I missed reading to her. The next morning when I went to wake her, she jumped up and said, "Hey, where were you last night? You didn't read the Buttstain Bears to me."

I said, "I'm sorry sweetheart, but I'm behind at the office and had to stay late to catch up."

Unfortunately, I had to work late that night also and missed reading to her again. The next morning when I went to wake her, she jumped up and said, "You weren't home again last night either! Why not?"

I said, "Sorry angel, but I'm still behind at the office and had to stay late to catch up!"

That night I had to work late again. The next morning when I woke her she asked, "Are you still behind at the office?" I said, "Yes!" She jumped out of bed, headed for the bathroom and without even looking back at me said. "Why don't they just put you in the slow group?"

The best know there must be balance in life. There must be a balance between work, home, spirituality and play. They all talk about the necessity of balance. They're the first to admit they may not have achieved that balance, but all insist they're working on it.

Set measurable goals and continuously stay focused

At the 2004 Summer Olympic Games in Athens, Greece, Mathew Emmons was about to fire his last shot in the rifle competition and secure winning the gold medal. He was in the lead, and all he needed on his last shot was a score of 7.2 to win gold. Up until this point his lowest score had been a 9.3.

He took aim, fired and hit the bull's eye. The only problem was that Emmons' shot hit the bull's eye on the wrong target. Instead of hitting the target in his lane, he hit the target in the lane next to him. Italy took the gold medal and Emmons ended up in eighth place. Emmons was devastated.

In an interview after the event, Emmons said he normally sighted the target number through his rifle's viewfinder first, then he would lower the gun to the bull's eye and shoot. He said he was nervous and did *not* do that on his last shot.

It doesn't matter how hard you work or how much you accomplish if you're not focused on the right targets.

Closing skills

The best match their products to their prospects identified needs. They listen carefully to make sure they've identified the right product that satisfies a real need. They're careful to make sure all questions have been answered and the cost of the solution is worth the investment on the customer's part.

When they're sure they close.

I held a focus group in Boca Raton, Fla. with 10 of the best salespeople at BellSouth Mobility. One of the sales representatives said, "Closing, when the time is right, is the most important part of the sales process. Closing is the secret to my success. Realizing that changed me from good to great in terms of sales results. I learned it one Saturday morning about three years ago. I wanted a new BMW 325 for years. I had money in my savings account, all my bills were paid, I owned a nice house and I was financially comfortable. I had been to the BMW dealership every Saturday for a month. My sales representative called me on Friday and told me the exact car I wanted had arrived. I got up Saturday and was at the dealership before it opened, checkbook in my back pocket. I drove it, we negotiated the price and I was ready to sign. My salesperson pulled the paperwork together and asked me to come in and sit down. Suddenly, pen in hand, I was having second thoughts. I had the money. I wasn't risking anything; it wasn't a 7 series for crying out loud, it was just a little 325. But I just couldn't take the next step and sign. Even when everything is right, no one wants to let go of that much money when they're just about to spend it. I put the pen down and told my salesperson I needed to think about it."

He said, "OK, I understand. Give me a call when you've decided."

"What I learned," said my top 10 percent sales representative, "was that even when everything is right people don't want to part with their money. If you, the sales representative, have listened well, provided the right product, right solution and the right price, you owe it to yourself *and* your customer to close the sale. Had my salesperson reviewed those facts with me and asked me to sign the order, I would have. I just needed a review and a push."

Many times an attempt to close will expose concerns that can be addressed. Other times an attempted close will bring up a concern that isn't really a concern at all but will help you determine what the real issue might be.

Years ago at AT&T when I was a new sales representative, I was sent to Denver, Co. for advanced sales training. I was one in a group of hundreds who were being prepared to sell AT&T's new telephone and computer products.

The training center was a large, odd-shaped, black, glass building that was known fondly throughout all of AT&T as Darth Vader University. We were there for three weeks and trained in all facets of selling to large accounts in our assigned industry segments.

The training was divided into 12 sections, and you had to certify in each of the 12 sections by passing an exam on that section. If you didn't pass any one of the sections after three attempts, you were sent back to your sales manager for "career planning." "Career planning" meant you were told by your boss to "plan on having a career somewhere else."

Module 11 was "Constructing the Solution and Development of the Proposal." In reality, we were supposed to be working independently on the proposal throughout the week, but almost everyone put it off until the end. I, being an overachiever and, using the formal title given to me by my classmates, "suck-up," had completed my proposal early and was the first to turn it into the instructor. The next morning, "Dan is a suck-up!" was scrawled on the white board!

I know you're all thinking that classmates can be cruel, but it was the instructor's handwriting!

The last section was the final exam, and we had to present our proposal to the customer. AT&T believed in making the experience as close to real-world as possible. The goal was to prepare the sales representatives for competitive selling. As a result, the folks who played the customers were actually retired CEOs and presidents from various large companies.

In my proposal presentation, I thought I was doing fine until the end when I was supposed to use my expert closing skills and get the customer's signature. He had apparently heard of my "title" and reputation, therefore he decided to make it hard on me.

I need to stop here and tell you that in order to pass the exam, we had to get the customer's signature. If the customer (the fake customer, retired CEO, real-world tough guy) made the determination that you didn't have a "cost justified" solution or your products weren't going to meet their needs, they wouldn't sign the order form at the back of the proposal.

We were told the "three attempts" rule didn't necessarily apply for the final exam. You could be sent home if you failed the final exam without being given a second or third chance. And, if the customer didn't sign and you failed, you could be sent home that night.

So, I sat there using every closing skill I had ever learned trying to get my CEO – who looked like Burt Reynolds, sounded like Bill Clinton, but used words like Donald Trump – to sign my order. I wasn't planning on going home to "plan my new career."

My CEO abruptly told me he couldn't sign as the decision needed board of directors' approval. I asked him when the board of directors met and his answer was "Not today, young man." Knowing that the "Plan your Career" flights were that evening, I told him, "It will take 10 days to process the order, so I'll write "subject to board approval" at the bottom. If the board doesn't approve the order, we have plenty of time to cancel it."

I wrote that statement at the bottom of the order form and turned it back around for his signature. In his Bill Clinton voice he said, "Well, it needs approval from my finance director before it goes to the board, and he's skiing in Aspen this week."

I then wrote "subject to approval of finance director." at the bottom and turned it back around for his signature. He looked at me and said, "Sir, the point is I'm not really sure this proposal meets our needs."

I took the proposal back and wrote "subject to being SURE" at the bottom under the other two contingencies. He exploded in laughter and signed the order.

Follow up on everything

Jim worked for a major telecommunications firm selling large telephone systems to medium-sized businesses. Jim had established his annual income goal to be $100,000 the year I interviewed him. His base salary was $50,000.

Jim knew it was going to take about an average of two weeks to close each sale and that he earned $2,300 average commission per sale. He calculated that he had 48 selling weeks a year taking holidays and vacation time into account. Jim also knew he had a 20 percent cancellation rate on the systems he sold, which was about average for the company.

Based on these facts, Jim calculated that his commission for the year would be $44,160. When added to his $50,000 base salary, he would fall short of his income goal by $5,840. Jim had never missed a sales quota or his annual income goals.

The new compensation plan paid about the same as it had for the last two years, but the sales cycle had been increasing each year. It took longer to make a sale because systems had increased in price, technology improvements and new features required the customer to make more upfront decisions, and many new competitors emerged.

Jim didn't want to miss his income goal, so he thought through his options. He could go ask for a raise. That was an unlikely solution! He then figured out he needed to sell two and a half more systems throughout the year to make up the difference. That was probably more unlikely than getting a raise. The sales cycle couldn't easily be reduced, and he would need four more weeks in the year to sell those two and a half additional systems. He could give up holidays and his vacation time to give him additional selling time, but that wasn't realistic either. Unless he could get his customers to give up their holidays and vacations, they wouldn't be there for him to sell to!

Then he had an idea. He could attempt to reduce the historical 20 percent cancellation rate on systems that were sold. He began to research why customers cancel in the first place.

Why do people cancel?

Buyer's remorse. Sometimes customers simply change their minds. Either they reconsider whether they can afford what they've just bought or they realize they really don't need it.

They continue shopping. Often after a customer buys something they'll continue shopping and find the same or similar item at a better price. Or they'll find another similar item that better fits their needs.

The product doesn't do what it's supposed to do. After the purchased item arrives it's determined that it doesn't perform as expected and doesn't solve the problem.

Doesn't solve the problem. The product performs exactly as it's supposed to do but doesn't solve the problem.

The customer doesn't do what they were supposed to do. There are times when the customer has to do certain things in advance of delivery of a product. If the customer doesn't take care of the advance work, the product may not function as required.

It's defective. It doesn't work and the customer doesn't get immediate satisfaction.

It's late. The customer had expectations on delivery and they weren't met.

The sales representative disappears. The sales representative convinces the customer that this was the right solution, but then can't be easily found. The customer has questions, second thoughts or concerns that go unanswered.

Jim decided based on his research that he could impact the cancellation rate. He decided the solution was to get out in front of those issues and manage the order processing all the way through delivery, installation and training. He created a follow-up plan and listed everything that needed to happen after he closed an average sale. Then he determined who had responsibility for each of those steps in the process.

This list began with the order processing steps and any potential delays that could impact the processing. Also included were the manufacturing steps and any potential problems that might affect the schedule. He also included the method of shipping and the time until receipt. The installation process, customer training schedule and the responsibilities the customer had prior to delivery and installation were also included.

Finally, Jim created a spreadsheet that listed all of these items, the time required for each and the people responsible for each step. He then determined routine and frequent follow-up dates and critical dates for each of the items listed. Each day he would start by reviewing all of the check points and critical dates for each sale in progress. He would make frequent yet brief contact with everyone who had responsibility for fulfillment of the order, including the customer. He had created his own project management process.

The result of managing the process, rather than letting it manage itself, was that his cancellation rate was reduced by half that first year. This allowed him to retain an additional $5,520 and took his total earnings to $99,680 for the year. Beyond Jim's income improvement, however, the real success story here was that customer satisfaction improved dramatically. Customer satisfaction improved both externally and internally as his co-workers appreciated his attention and help.

The Customer Experience Commitment of the Top 10 Percent

I'm surprised when I'm treated well when buying a product or service these days. It doesn't happen as often as it used to ... being treated well, that is. It appears to me that salespeople in general have forgotten it's my money and they should be attentive, appreciative and nice in order to get me to spend it with them. Perhaps they haven't forgotten anything. It may be that they know I'll spend it with them regardless of how they treat me.

I went out to buy myself a new computer recently. I didn't buy one that day and still haven't bought one. I know exactly what I want, and I can even order it over the Hewlett-Packard website, but I won't. I may even be able to buy it online cheaper, but I won't. "Dan, why have you not bought a new computer yet?" you might be asking about now. The answer is I've not yet found the right salesperson. I know what features and software I want, and I know what accessories I need. I have no questions. I'm simply waiting for the right salesperson.

The right salesperson is the one who will greet me and stay with me without running off every time his or her clip-on walkie-talkie calls out begging for attention. The right salesperson will have my best interest in mind. The right salesperson will be a top 10 percent salesperson. I hope I find the right salesperson tonight because I really need a new computer. I believe my old one is haunted. It makes noises and stuff pops up even when I'm not touching it. Much of what it does while I'm using it scares me.

The best salespeople still believe the customer is the priority. They still believe the customer is the reason they have a job, an income, and the reason for which their company exists. And they know their past and future success rests in the customer's hands.

Customer experience

- **The customer is always "the customer"**
- **The customer takes priority over all else**
- **Break the "Golden Rule"**
- **Always be there on time**
- **Follow up to ensure no surprises**
- **Adapt to the customer**
- **Customers buy me, the company and the experience**

The customer is always "the customer"

The best all say something along the lines of *the customer is always the customer*. They may say it a bit differently, but the general sentiment is the same. These are our customers, the people we serve, and we'll treat them as such always. They deserve our respect, full attention and the highest level of care, always.

The best salespeople don't use the old saying, "the customer is always right" because they aren't always right. They're sometimes wrong like everyone else. That doesn't mean it's important to tell the customer they're wrong, it simply means that sometimes their opinion may differ from that of the sales representative. And if it does, remember they are still the customer and need to be treated with the highest regard and respect.

I've always dug a bit deeper on this issue and asked the best salespeople what they do when the customer is wrong. The answer is always about the same. If the customer is wrong about something that isn't related to the transaction or how the product will perform to meet the customer's expectations, why challenge them? The fact that the customer doesn't believe that the Waffle House serves the best breakfast in town should not be a reason to treat a customer with disrespect. Now, if it were me, I would drag the heathen customer to the nearest Waffle House for a bacon and cheese omelet with scattered and covered hash browns. The best, however, say they diplomatically overlook such obviously incorrect opinions.(The best salespeople must be made of steel to overlook that opinion.)

On the other hand, if the customer is wrong about something that will result in a severe problem related to the use of the product, it needs to be diplomatically addressed. Let's say that a customer states that they're buying a child seat to put in the front seat of their minivan, despite the warnings all over the box. The salesperson needs to be diplomatic, but must point out that use of the seat in this manner can result in injury or death.

The customer takes priority over all else

When I was in college, I worked at JCPenney's in the shoe department. The day I was hired, the store manager made it a point to come meet me. He said two things to me I'll never forget.

"Welcome to JCPenney's," he said. "We're glad you came to work here."

Then he pointed to a tile on the floor and said, "This is your floor tile. If you're not waiting on a customer or straightening the sales floor from your last customer, I expect to see you standing on it waiting for your next customer to walk in. We're here for the customers. They're of utmost importance. We don't hang out in the stockroom or cluster together and chat when we're not waiting on customers. Once we've cleaned up from the last customer, we stand and wait for the next customer to walk in."

In an earlier chapter I talked about a meeting I held with the top 10 sales representatives from our sales force in Miami. I was holding a session like so many I held before where I brought the best together to share their views on their success. One salesperson made the comment that the customer was the No. 1 priority. Some of the comments from the other salespeople were, "It's all about them, and I'm in the moment with them."

"This is their time with me and my company, and I give them my full attention." "Even if the boss calls, I will tell her I have to call back because I'm with a customer." "I let nothing interrupt. They're the reason I have a job. If they need me I'm there." "The customer is of utmost importance."

Incidentally, this meeting took all day because we kept losing salespeople when their customers would call them on their cellular phones. It took us an hour just to get all 10 of them together for a photo.

Break the "Golden Rule"

That rule of course is, *Do unto others as you would have them do unto you.* The best disregard and break that rule. They consciously don't treat the customer as they would themselves want to be treated. They treat the customer the way the customer wants to be treated. You'll recall in the chapter on mindset I said that "right the first time" was a practice and not just a statement. The same applies to "break the golden rule." It's a practice, not simply a statement.

How is it put into practice? First, listen well to fully and completely understand what the customer's needs are. The next step is to ask questions to better determine what product or service will best satisfy those needs. It helps to ask the customer what they expect in terms of a solution and how they see your product helping them. Finally, confirm your understanding of the expectations with the customer. In the end, it's all about the customer's expectations of how you, your company and products will help them or satisfy a need.

Always be there on time

I spent a great deal of time earlier discussing the importance of *being there*. I dealt with *being there* as a disciplined action of the best related to prospecting for new business. Simply stated, if you're where the customers are and ready to work, you'll be successful. If, on the other hand, you're sitting in a bean bag watching *Wheel of Fortune,* you won't.

Now let's look at the other side of being there on time, the customer side. The best salespeople are fanatical about being on time. When I spent time with the best they were crazy-nuts about leaving in plenty of time to get

The Customer Experience Commitment of the Top 10 Percent

to appointments. I felt like I did when I was a kid on a field trip to Washington, D.C. and the nuns chased me continuously to move to the next monument in a timely manner.

At one point BellSouth owned a business in London, and I was sent there to rebuild the sales organization. I had a sales representative who was insane about being on time. He had a very long and hyphenated last named that I screwed up continuously so most of the time I called him Clopsey. Now don't get me wrong, I'm seldom, if ever, late. But Clopsey was 45 minutes early to every appointment to prevent from being late.

Clopsey's territory was downtown London, and I would often make sales calls with him. We both lived outside the city, so we would meet somewhere on the outskirts of town and ride into London together. London traffic is horrible. The closer you get to the downtown area, the slower it gets until it comes to a crawl and then just stops. When the traffic began to crawl, Clopsey panicked. When he started to panic, Clopsey would simply pull over and park. We would walk to the nearest tube (subway) station and ride the rest of the way downtown. We were never late to an appointment. At the end of the day, we would ride the tube back to the station where we left the car and go home.

Except for one day!

It was Wimbledon week and traffic was crazy everywhere. Not much was moving. Clopsey tried two or three alternate routes, panicked, pulled over and down into the tube we went. Late that afternoon when we were finished, we got on the tube to head home when suddenly Clopsey realized he didn't remember which station we had parked near. He didn't even remember which tube line it was on. After about two hours of popping up at every station we came to, we took the train to *my* car, which was parked near Windsor. The next day we took my car, drove into town and retraced our route until we found his car, parked where we had left it with one of those yellow boot things locked to the front wheel.

Follow up to ensure no surprises

I bought a house in South Florida from a realtor who was full of surprises. I can't tell the story because I've blocked it from my mind. Suffice to say, it was the worst purchase experience of my life. I *will* tell you about the last surprise because it was a classic. The closing was over and the realtor said he would meet us at the house. He went ahead while we stopped to get lunch. When we arrived at the house, we pulled the van into the garage, shut the garage door and headed for the door to go inside. I noticed it was a really tight fit for the van in the garage. Later, I would learn that the unusual size of the lot required the garage to be built a bit smaller than most houses. Allow me to go back to the last surprise. I grabbed the door knob, turned it and pushed the door. It wouldn't open.

Then I heard my realtor say, from inside the house, "Oh, I forgot to tell you hurricane code requires that all doors open out rather than in."

Then the door opened about three inches and slammed into the bumper of the van. I was quite certain even my smallest child couldn't fit through that opening and said so to the realtor, whose nose I could see poking through the tiny little opening.

He said, "Looks like you'll need to park on the other side of the garage."

"That's fine until we get the other car here," I said.

OK, I'm going to end the story here; it only gets worse and I want to keep it blocked out of my head!

The importance of follow up has already been covered in Chapter 9 under sales actions. The no surprises piece is the take away from the best here. In interviews the best routinely say it's very important that the customer's expectations be met. Avoid any surprises by following up!

Don't you hate the closing process when you buy a house? I've never understood the truth in lending statements, the closing estimate cost sheet and the 6,312 other pieces of paper your realtor gives you prior to the closing. And while we're talking about realtors, why do all realtors have pictures of themselves on their business cards that were taken 20 years ago? There needs to be federal regulation related to realtor business cards like there is on automobile passenger rear view mirrors. Just like where it says OBJECTS IN MIRROR MAY BE CLOSER THAN THEY APPEAR, a realtor's business card needs to have a warning that reads, REALTOR IN PICTURE MAY BE OLDER THAN APPEARS. My point is that there are always surprises at closing. The need for a termite inspection letter, the cost for the extra stuff you got on the pool that wasn't included in the financing of the house, the seven-year prepaid insurance policy – all surprises!

The best follow up routinely to provide status to the customer, reinforce their purchase decision and remind them of anything they need to do in advance of delivery.

In a retail store where purchases are immediate, the best take care to detail everything for the customer in terms of return policies, warranties and operation of their new purchase. In addition, the best retail salespeople take it a step further and follow up after the sale to make sure the customer is satisfied and to remind them of the policies, warranties, etc.

Adapt to the customer

Recall that in Chapter 6 we covered the fact that the best have a "think like the customer" mindset. The best adapt to the customer. They say it in many different ways, but my trusty thesaurus led me to the word "adapt."

A thesaurus is a dictionary of synonyms and antonyms…hmmmm. A book in which you find other words for words. Don't you find it a bit ironic there's no other word for thesaurus?

Adapting to the customer may sometimes require more than just listening. Sometimes adjusting to different conditions may be required to ensure that we understand and satisfy the customer's needs. When I was with BellSouth Mobility, I was visiting my retail stores one day with the president of BellSouth Enterprises. He came down to South Florida from Atlanta and was having a real problem with the approach that Ken, a sales representative, was taking with a customer.

Every once in a while, Ken would speak a bit harshly to the customer and say something like, "You don't need that; this is what you need." Or, "No, that won't work either, you have to buy this one."

The customer, an elderly gentleman with a New York accent, was arguing back with Ken, and they were interrupting each other constantly.

My boss whispered to me that we needed to get rid of Ken as he was entirely too rude to the customers. I commented that he had just returned from our annual sales conference where he was recognized as one of the top 10 salespeople in the company and that I was as shocked as he was.

As the little old man passed us on the way out the door, he stopped and said to us, "You two muck-adee-mucks look like the bosses. I want to tell you something about that guy!" He then pointed his crooked finger at my sales representative and said, "Ken is the best salesperson I ever met and the reason I stay with your company." Then he hobbled out the door.

We stood there watching Ken take on a completely different tone with another gentleman. He became respectfully quiet, listened well and finally said, "Based on where you travel and how you plan to use your phone, let me recommend this one."

When things died down a bit, I said to Ken that I was afraid he and the old gentleman were really arguing. Ken leaned over the counter, looked me square in the eyes, smiled and said, "You gotta talk like your customers. They come in for a phone, but they stay with us for the experience."

Customers buy me, the company and the experience.

While out in Salt Lake City at an annual sales recognition event, I cornered one of the top salespeople being honored. During our conversation about why he was one of the best he said, "Customers aren't buying a product, they're buying how they want to feel. And they're buying from me based on their experience with me and the reputation of the company I represent."

There's little I can say to add any value to that statement. Although expressed in a variety of ways by others, the above quote truly captures the essence of the best salespeople's feelings about what customers buy. They tell us people aren't really buying a thing so much as they're buying a solution to a problem, satisfaction of a need or to experience a specific emotion. The product or service is the vehicle to achieve these.

Why Are the Best Motivated to Be So Successful?

Why do the best salespeople want to be the best? Why do they care? Certainly many will admit they are motivated by money, but that isn't the sole reason. A good salesperson can earn a strong income in sales without having to be the best in the company. So, why are the people I've talked with so driven to be in the top 10 percent?

Up until this point we've been talking about what the best do to be the best. Now let's explore why?

Motivation

- **Money**
- **Recognition**
- **Competition**
- **Advancement**
- **Pride and self-satisfaction**
- **Control**
- **Fear of failure**

Money

Money is the No. 1 motivator for the best salespeople. The ability to control their own income and have the things they need and want in life while building financial independence drives the top 10 percent.

A sales representative in San Diego said to me, "Money won't buy happiness, but I'm happy to just rent some of it for the afternoon when I'm out on my boat."

Recognition and achievement

Being recognized as the best of the best is another top reason these excellent salespeople are so driven. They're driven to achieve and want to be recognized and congratulated for having accomplished extraordinary results.

They're exhilarated by that feeling of accomplishment and pride when their peers, managers and families acknowledge that they're among the very best. Recognition events are extremely important to salespeople, but they are absolutely essential to the best ones.

They proudly display every top honor they ever achieved for all to see. Recall the words of my first manager at Motorola, "If you can't pay 'em, plaque 'em!"

Competition

The best are highly competitive and driven to surpass others. This doesn't mean that top 10 percent salespeople paint their faces with company colors and greet everyone in the break room with high fives and body slams. It *does* mean they strive to attain goals and surpass others attempting to attain the same goals. You'll find that many competitive people aren't obvious about it.

I'm a runner. I run alone four days a week. I run an average of 24.8 miles a week, which equates to four 10K runs a week. I'll be the first to say I don't feel the need to run races and compete to beat others. I'm happy to run alone just for the feeling of accomplishment at having achieved my weekly goal of 24.8 miles. But, let me come upon another runner when I'm out running alone! Or, just let another runner sneak up behind me as

I'm out running alone! I'll kill myself to ensure I pass the runner in front of me or that no other runner passes me. Just let them try to block me with their kid's strollers or throw their oxygen tanks at me; I'm passing anyway.

Advancement

While many of the best are very, very happy in their roles as excellent, well-paid and recognized salespeople, there are many who want advancement. So why is someone who wants to advance within a company driven to be the best in sales? It's because achieving best-of-the-best status in sales gives you high visibility. It's an excellent way to be recognized and distinguish yourself from the crowd.

Many excellent salespeople came into sales with a goal of advancement to general management and not simply sales management. When I graduated from college, my father told me a position in sales was the best place to be to advance within a company. He said in addition to it being a high-visibility position, it was the best place to learn all about a company. In sales you interface with all of the departments, and the more you know about the whole company, the better for advancement.

Pride and self-satisfaction

The best of the best are very proud of their accomplishments. We all are proud of what we accomplish, but some of the best feel a very strong sense of pride, self-satisfaction and value in their accomplishments. Sales provides an atmosphere for these individuals to flourish.

I had a college professor who once told the class he felt a great sense of self satisfaction in what he had accomplished after he cut his lawn. But he said he only felt that pride when it was very evident he had cut it. For that reason, he would only cut it every other week. That way the accomplishment was quite evident and his sense of pride amplified. I always thought he was just lazy!

The independent nature of sales provides clear sight of what has been accomplished. And that clear sight allows value, satisfaction and pride to easily be felt from what has been accomplished.

Control

I once had the opportunity to spend an evening with a gentleman who had been held as a prisoner of war for many years. I heard him speak many times about his experience, but that evening I was able to talk to him one-on-one about it. He related to me that one of the worst parts of the experience was that he had no control over anything.

I'm certainly not, in any way, trying to compare our daily struggles in the sales world with the experience of a prisoner of war. My only point is that the need to have control over our own environment is very strong. Some seek out positions in sales because the job is one where they can have a great degree of control. Many jobs don't offer the ability to control your daily activities as much as in sales. And that control provides the freedom to set and accomplish your own goals.

Fear of failure

And last but certainly not least is the fear of failure. There were some top 10 percent salespeople who told me their strongest motivation was born out of a fear of failure. They would set aggressive goals, work long hours, measure themselves against all those around them obsessively in order to avoid the possibility of failure. Most times the result was over performance.

So What?

I once made a presentation on how the top 10 percent in sales got there to a mixed group of people from outside sales, retail sales, telesales and some who were purely customer service people. The presentation went very well with everyone taking notes and asking questions at the end. I felt very good about the feedback and comments that followed.

One gentleman had waited patiently, however, and when everyone else left the room he came up to me and said, "Dan, that's great about the top 10 percent and all that, but so what if these people are successful in sales! I don't want to be in sales. I'm happy with my life and job in customer service now. And I have balance. I have my family, church and hobbies, and I coach sports. So, why should I care if they want to be at the top in sales? I'm happy with where I am now, and there's more to life than being a successful sales representative."

I realized that my message wasn't as clear as I thought. Certainly the sales representatives had gained tremendous insight into the character and practices of the very best, but weren't there other lessons to be learned? Was there no relevance between the practices that make one successful in sales and those needed in other jobs or other aspects of life?

You see, it has always been my opinion that we're all in sales. Not just at work but in all aspects of life. A definition of sales being:

Sell. *verb***,** sold, sell – ing, *noun – verb* used with object.
4. To persuade another to recognize the worth or desirability of:

I've always felt the character and attributes of the best in sales can serve as an example for all of us regardless of what our jobs are. After all, given the definition of sales, aren't we all trying to persuade others to see the worth or desirability of our positions related to various issues every day?

Doesn't a teacher use persuasive skills to help students see the desirability of learning? Is a doctor or nurse not educating their patients to recognize the value of exercise and of eating healthy? The politician, the lawyer, your mother and father, the preacher or priest in your church, aren't they all persuading?

I see strong relevance and application for what we can learn from the character, attributes and practices of the top 10 performers in any work group. This book just happens to be on those top performers in sales.

And if we review what we learned about the character of the top 10 percent in sales – friendly, outgoing, determined, persistent, confident, independent, team member, passionate and honest – aren't those attributes that would serve any of us well in all aspects of life?

My position then would be that these very good and strong sales representatives, who I've had the pleasure to learn from, are simply very good and strong people.

About the Author

Dan Norman has hired, developed and managed countless top 10% sales performers throughout his career and he knows from experience the fundamental work that it takes to get there. Dan understands what the top 10% do to exceed expectations, the mechanics of how they do it and how they stay at that level year after year.

Dan has more than 25 years of experience serving most recently as Vice President and General Manager over one of the largest markets at Cingular Wireless (now at&t). He has built and led large and successful sales organizations in the United States and the United Kingdom and has hired and motivated thousands of sales representatives. His experience covers all sales channels, including outside business to business sales, major accounts, retail sales and telemarketing sales.

During his educational, informative and humorous keynote presentations, Dan examines and teaches the proven fundamentals for getting to and staying in the top 10%. He underscores the fundamentals through a combination of relatable stories and specific examples to assure that his audience fully understands and remembers the key takeaways.

Importantly, Dan completes his advance homework to assure that he understands the products, competition and challenges faced by his client. He then uses this knowledge to customize his presentation so that the audience better understands how to apply the fundamentals in their own workplace.

Contact
Dan Norman

To reserve a date for Dan to speak at your next event or for additional information, you can reach him at :

Dan Norman
P.O. Box 470416
Celebration, FL 34747
(407) 760-1000

Email: dan@toptenselling.com
Website: www.toptenselling.com